Three Adventist Titans:

The Significance of Heeding or Rejecting the Counsel of Ellen White

By Albert Dittes

TEACH Services, Inc.
PUBLISHING
www.TEACHServices.com • (800) 367-1844

World rights reserved. This book or any portion thereof may not be copied or reproduced in any form or manner whatever, except as provided by law, without the written permission of the publisher, except by a reviewer who may quote brief passages in a review.

This book was written to provide truthful information in regard to the subject matter covered. The author assumes full responsibility for the accuracy of all facts and quotations as cited in this book. The opinions expressed in this book are the author's personal views and interpretation of the Bible, Spirit of Prophecy, and/or contemporary authors and do not necessarily reflect those of TEACH Services, Inc.

This book is sold with the understanding that the publisher is not engaged in giving spiritual, legal, medical, or other professional advice. If authoritative advice is needed, the reader should seek the counsel of a competent professional.

Copyright © 2013 TEACH Services, Inc.
ISBN-13: 978-1-4796-0038-0 (Paperback)
ISBN-13: 978-1-4796-0039-7 (ePub)
ISBN-13: 978-1-4796-0040-3 (Kindle/Mobi)
Library of Congress Control Number: 2013934650

Published by

www.TEACHServices.com • (800) 367-1844

Table of Contents

Preface — 5

Digressing From the Vision — 7

A Profile of John Harvey Kellogg: A Ministry Without Ministers — 15

A Profile of Arthur G. Daniells: A Ministry Without Physicians — 43

A Profile of Percy T. Magan: A Ministry Built Around Ellen White — 69

Getting Back To The Vision — 101

Preface

Several years ago, while working in the Center for Adventist Research at Andrews University, I found a booklet of correspondence penned by Percy T. Magan.

I had heard his name all my life since my father had gone to medical school at Loma Linda when he was president there. I also knew that he had cofounded Madison College near Nashville, Tennessee, which was about thirty-five miles from where I grew up. My grandfather's first cousin, Frances Dittes, taught there under him and his close friend E. A. Sutherland and she often talked about him.

Much of his correspondence included letters exchanged with Lida Funk Scott, another name familiar to me. I had known of her as a wealthy woman who had dedicated her share of the Funk & Wagnalls fortune to the work of Madison and Loma Linda through the influence of E. A. Sutherland. But I did not know that she had left such a big mark on the denomination through her financial support until I read these letters.

Being a master fund-raiser, Magan kept her informed of what was going on at Loma Linda, which included telling her about the people giving him a hard time.

I knew I had found a treasure trove of Adventist history, and I developed this correspondence into a book entitled *Letters from Dr. Percy Magan*, showing the trials and tribulations involved in developing The College of Medical Evangelists into a Grade A medical school.

Once completed, I heard some unusual responses to this book. Several Adventist medical professionals said it illustrated how hard it was for physicians to work with the denomination.

Their comments inspired me to go to the root of the Adventist medical/ministerial division by profiling three prominent founders—John Harvey Kellogg, Arthur G. Daniells and Percy Magan—of the present system and their relationships with Ellen White.

I have always viewed Ellen White as a prophetess who was given divine instruction for our church, but I wanted to find out firsthand how these men felt about her. I, therefore, read their correspondence with Ellen White and looked closely for clues as to how their minds worked and their attitude to the gift of prophecy. Their letters tell the story of how the dedicated Adventist ministers and physicians at the highest levels—especially Kellogg and Daniells—could never quite work together hand in hand in proclaiming the three angels' messages to the world, while Magan followed her counsel to the fullest extent.

A look at their correspondence shows they all believed in Ellen White and followed most of her advice. She had a role in making all of them prominent, but that did not necessarily make it easy to follow all of the directions.

Their letters to Ellen White tell in rich detail their visions for the church and what they were up against. All three enlarged the work they inherited from the Adventist pioneers. Their generation made the Seventh-day Adventist Church a major evangelical movement with conferences and institutions all over the world.

The staff of the Ellen G. White Estate at the General Conference headquarters and the branch office at Oakwood University in Huntsville, Alabama, have been most helpful in my research. In particular, I thank Tim Poirier of the home office in Silver Spring, Maryland, and Jonathan Thompson and Tonya Loveday at Oakwood for their assistance in finding this invaluable correspondence.

I am also indebted to the Adventist Archives Web site for having every edition of the *Review and Herald*, starting with the *Present Truth* in 1849, online. Using their search engine, I accessed *Review* articles by and about these three individuals, revealing their convictions as well as tracing their career highlights.

Their leadership and life decisions teach us many lessons about what happens when directions from the Spirit of Prophecy are and are not followed. My goal and prayer is that our present generation will learn from those who have gone before us to bring their great work to a glorious climax.

Albert Dittes
Portland, Tennessee

Digressing From the Vision

A wedding in Battle Creek, Michigan, on June 15, 1898, united two prominent families and demonstrated how respectable Adventism had become in the community. The local newspaper described it as "one of the prettiest and most elaborate weddings of the season."

The bride, Vera Brackett, was not only the daughter of Mr. and Mrs. Charles Brackett, prosperous local farmers, but she was also the niece of brothers W. K. and Dr. John Harvey Kellogg. The groom, Dr. John Byington, was also from a prominent Adventist family. One of his relatives had served as the first president of the General Conference.

Both families had moved to Battle Creek about the time the headquarters of the struggling young church settled there in 1855. Uriah Smith, editor of the Review and Herald and another well-known Adventist, united the couple in marriage. "Elder Smith was led to refer tenderly and feelingly to the pleasant relations that had existed between himself and the parents and grandparents of both parties, extending over a period of nearly half a century," commented the newspaper.

The pioneer struggles were over by now, and the guests enjoyed a wedding ceremony in a "commodious home beautifully decorated with flowers, ferns and potted plants, and the spacious lawn lighted with Japanese lanterns. About one hundred and twenty guests were present, quite a number coming from a distance."

Not in attendance was Ellen G. White. She was living in Australia at the time, while Battle Creek flourished and grew, resulting in many Adventists living quite comfortably. Mrs. White had counseled the church that it should operate small sanitariums in many places, but Kellogg knew he could attract many patients from all over the world to one place, so he disregarded her guidance. He had also spawned a breakfast food industry with Charles W. Post, who had already become a multimillionaire by selling breakfast foods. His brother, W. K. Kellogg, soon followed suit and entered the food manufacturing business.

Although James and Ellen White had started the Review and Herald, with great sacrifice, to proclaim the three angels' messages, the publishing house in Battle Creek had developed into one of the biggest and best of its kind in the state through printing commercial literature. Ellen White strongly opposed this practice as well as the high salaries its top officers were making. Furthermore, she advised against the investment of large sums of money to enlarge Battle Creek College, thus attracting Adventist families to the area.

Typifying these better things now within reach of the Adventist families in the area, young John Byington had gone to medical school and soon became a prominent physician at the Battle Creek Sanitarium until his premature death in 1911 at the age of 39.

"Dr. Byington is a specialist and is in charge of the ear, eye, nose and throat department at the Sanitarium, and has already earned an enviable reputation for his skill in this line," stated the news account. "Mrs. Byington has for some time taught in the public schools of the county, and among her many attainments is an accomplished musician."

An obituary of Vera Byington described her education as having been in the "Marshall schools and this was supplemented by attendance at Olivet College and the University of Michigan, she having attended the University School of Music, where she cultivated her voice that made her prominent in musical circles both in college and private life."

"This marriage unites nearly forty families prominent in the denomination of which they are members," the account mentioned.

The news article went on to describe the attire of the bridal party. "The beautiful and accomplished bride was attired in a gown of rich cream satin, trimmed with point-lace and pearl pasamenterie, and carried a boquet [sic] of white roses. The groom was dressed in the conventional black.

"Immediately after congratulations, which were profuse and hearty, the guests viewed the wedding presents which were numerous and valuable. Among them was a silk-knit purse containing twenty $5 gold pieces and a telegram of congratulation from Dr. J. H. Kellogg, who is at present on the Pacific coast."[1]

Adventism had indeed arrived in Battle Creek, which Ellen White described as being "not the whole world." In addressing delegates at the 1901 General Conference session she said, "No, indeed. We have a world to save, and upon every one of us rests a most solemn responsibility. Let us stand in the counsel of God, in our lot and place, ready to help wherever help is needed … What does it mean that so many of our large cities are unworked? Have you been learning at the footstool of Jesus? Have the workers in our institutions been doing their duty? Have they been trying to advance the work of the Lord? God calls for workmen. He wants those who have gained an experience in the cause to enter the work in America. He wants them to take up the work in New York and in other cities where iniquity prevails."[2]

She spoke these words to a gathering of Adventists who were in the process of transforming from

---

1   "Wedding Bells, Byington-Brackett," June 15, 1898, Ross Coller Collection, Willard Library, Local History, Battle Creek, Michigan.

2   *Advent Review and Sabbath Herald*, April 10, 1901, p. 184.

a religious group spread across the United States into an international movement. During the past fifty-seven years, missionary-minded Adventists had made impressive strides forward from New England and moving steadily westward, with headquarters in Rochester, New York, and later in Michigan. The message had then leapfrogged across the North American continent to the Pacific Coast and took root in the southeastern United States. Next it hopscotched across the Atlantic Ocean to Europe and penetrated deep into Russia. The church now needed a broader, more regional organization so that workers in Australia, India, South Africa, and the Orient did not need to consult with administrators at Battle Creek in order to resolve local issues.

A new generation assumed leadership of the Seventh-day Adventist Church as it began the twentieth century at this pivotal General Conference session in Battle Creek.

The pioneers had died or relinquished their responsibilities one by one. James White, J. N. Andrews, and Joseph Bates were gone, and Uriah Smith would soon follow. Ellen White had just returned from Australia to Elmshaven, California, where she planned to semi-retire.

It was at this General Conference session that three relatively young men, who had grown up under the pioneer influence, made themselves known. John Harvey Kellogg, forty-nine years old, had served as superintendent of the now world-famous Battle Creek Sanitarium for twenty-five years. He had enlarged the health ministry there into founding food companies and schools of medical science, training physicians and nurses. He would eventually part company with the denomination but would not be forgotten.

Arthur G. Daniells, forty-three years old and fresh from fourteen successful years of ministry in Australia and New Zealand, would take the leadership reins of the denomination and develop it into one of the great organizations in Christendom during the next twenty years.

Percy T. Magan, thirty-four years old, had served as a reform-minded college professor and dean at Battle Creek College for the past ten years as well as writing many books and articles. He would later take over leadership of the Adventist medical work from Kellogg by bringing the College of Medical Evangelists in Southern California to full respectability in the medical world. At this General Conference session, he served as a delegate-at-large, secretary of the Finance Committee, and member of the Publishing Committee and the General Conference Association Committee of 21. The Review advertised a pamphlet he had authored entitled "The Battle of the Century" treating "the great struggle for civil and religious liberty" by analyzing such subjects as Rome and the United States, the French Revolution, Napoleon and the pope, the deadly wound, and American Sunday Laws.

Daniells led out from the start. "We talk about the General Conference, but we have never had a General Conference," he said. "We have had a North American General Conference, or a North America Union Conference but we have not had a world's General Conference.... If Union Conferences are organized, a thousand details will be taken from the General Conference Committee, and placed in the hands of the local men, where they belong."[3]

---

3   *Advent Review and Sabbath Herald*, April 30, 1901, p. 8.

During the session a committee on organization recommended they first form the Southern Union Conference, then the Lake Union, and finally the Eastern and Pacific Unions. Daniells served as chair of this committee and became in effect president of the General Conference from then on though he did not immediately assume that title.

"I have no confidence in plans that leave the main decisions regarding the work in distant lands with a board in this country, whose members have never been on the ground," he added. "These men can not gather in an upper room here in Battle Creek, and intelligently plan the affairs of people in distant fields. It is not natural; it is not sensible. It must not be done."[4]

Daniells spent his years of service as president perfecting such an organization, dividing the world field into sectional unions. Then as the church grew to full maturity, he offered direction into splitting the church into larger regional divisions.

The delegates also considered a pressing problem of debt on Adventist schools. Ellen White had given the profit from her new book *Christ's Object Lessons* to relieve these school debts, and Magan led out in persuading church members to sell this book.

"The debts were forever increasing until … it seemed almost impossible that they should ever be paid," he said in describing the desperate situation.[5]

"A number of letters were written to Sister White upon the subject … The matter was quite thoroughly laid before her, and again and again she answered that she would be glad to send a ringing appeal to all our people to help to reduce these debts; but that the angel of the Lord restrained her from doing so until our schools adopted right principles."[6]

Magan and his close friend Edward A. Sutherland had led out in instituting educational reforms at Battle Creek College, and this had inspired Ellen White to devote the proceeds from *Christ's Object Lessons* to help revitalize the schools.

Magan reported a total of $15,936.02 in publishing costs, and he estimated the publishers had shipped out between 70,000 and 75,000 copies of *Christ's Object Lessons*. Union College sold 14,078 copies at $1.25 each, bringing them $17,722.40 in assistance. Battle Creek College netted $16,761.53 from the sale of 13,739 copies, While Walla Walla College and Mount Vernon Academy each reduced their debt by $4,000. The sale of *Christ's Object Lessons* also brought some relief to Keene Academy in Texas, Oakwood Industrial School in Alabama, and Southern Industrial School in Tennessee.[7]

Magan announced that the Battle Creek reforms had gone beyond the local campus into starting other schools elsewhere. "Sister White has kept sending testimonies to us that we must establish small industrial schools outside of Battle Creek in various Conferences of this district, in order that our youth of younger years, say from 15 to 18 years of age, might be educated in the country away from the cities, and away from the wrong influences and troubles which have grown up in this large and

---

4 Ibid.
5 *Advent Review and Sabbath Herald*, April 14, 1901, p. 210.
6 General Conference Bulletin, April 14, 1901, p. 210.
7 Ibid.

congested center," he said, referring to new schools in Woodland, Wisconsin; Cedar Lake, Michigan; and Sheridan, Illinois.

"These schools are small, are situated in the country, and are industrial in their nature, patterned, I believe, more largely after the Avondale school in Australia than any other class of schools among us," he continued. "You can readily see that will cut down the attendance at the school here in Battle Creek most materially; and from the light given us, that attendance ought to be cut down."

While admitting that lesser enrollment would mean fewer tuition dollars for Battle Creek College, Magan felt the right thing had been done.

"From the moral standpoint I don't know that I need to add any more than what has been so plainly stated in the Testimonies,—that the school would be infinitely better off if it were located outside of Battle Creek. Therefore, I believe that this body should seriously take under consideration the movement of the school from this place to a more favorable locality."[8]

The assembly authorized Magan and College President E. A. Sutherland to find such a rural location, and they opened the new school the next year in Berrien Springs, Michigan.

Ellen White endorsed this rural move. "God wants the school to be taken out of Battle Creek," she said. "Let us take away the excuse which has been made for families to come into Battle Creek.... The light that has been given me is that Battle Creek has not the best influence over the students in our school. There is altogether too congested a state of things. The school, although it will mean a fewer number of students, should be moved out of Battle Creek. Get an extensive tract of land, and there begin the work which I entreated should be commenced before our school was established here,—to get out of the cities, to a place where the students would not see things to remark upon and criticise, where they would not see the wayward course of this one and that one, but would settle down to diligent study."[9]

She also agreed with the plan of church members selling *Christ's Object Lessons* for more than one reason.

"It is the Lord's design that *Christ's Object Lessons*, with its precious instruction, will unify the believers. The self-sacrificing efforts put forth by the members of our churches will prove a means of uniting them, that they may be sanctified, body, soul, and spirit, as vessels unto honor, prepared to receive the Holy Spirit."

She continued, "Let the work of relieving our schools go steadily forward. Work to the point, and the blessing of God will rest upon you. And when the debt is lifted, still continue the work; for a fund should be raised to send to school students who can not pay their own way."[10]

Another big agenda item was the medical missionary work, which, under the leadership of Kellogg, had outstripped the entire denomination in some ways. W. W. Prescott was shocked to learn that the International Medical Missionary and Benevolent Association, which had been chartered eight

---

8   Ibid., p. 212.
9   Ibid., pp. 215, 216.
10 Ibid.

years before, employed more people than the entire denomination. Kellogg reported that 2,000 people worked under him, and Prescott noted that the General Conference employed 1,500 people.

Indeed, the medical work had grown to include eleven treatment rooms and twenty-seven sanitariums in the United States, Mexico, Great Britain, Denmark, India, South Africa, Switzerland, Samoa, and Germany.[11]

Kellogg also reported medical and nursing schools as well as a mission in Chicago ministering to "the poor and destitute." His work of reform included a health food company, which sold $1,000 a day in cereal foods.[12]

Dr. David Paulson told the delegates that the Chicago mission was reaching five classes of people: poverty-stricken, wager-earners, the "unfortunate class," criminals, and the wealthy. "As far as I am concerned personally, the two years I have spent in Chicago have been the happiest of my life," he added.[13]

Kellogg documented the oversized Battle Creek Sanitarium. "At the present time we have twenty buildings at the Sanitarium," he reported. "In addition to that we are occupying eighty cottages, besides the south dormitory of the college. I say we are occupying eighty buildings around town, which we rent, and we own twenty buildings at the Sanitarium. And they are all crowded full."[14]

Elder E. J. Hibbard, a minister on the sanitarium staff, spoke of the religious work being done there. "My observation is that it is all evangelical. I have observed quite closely the working of every department of the institution."

He reported patient requests for Bible studies, and all classes of patients studying the gospel. Several had accepted Adventism despite no attempts to proselyte.[15]

But what was being done there was not enough.

"Just as soon as possible let schools be established and workers educated to do medical missionary work," Ellen White said. "This work is the right hand of the body. It is bound up with the ministry of the gospel. God lives and reigns, and he desires those who have opposed health reform, who have worked against it by their influence, by their actions, by their sarcastic remarks, to make a thorough change. Do not divorce yourselves from the medical missionary work."[16]

She indicated that she had been given special light that those claiming to believe present truth should take up medical missionary work.

"How were they to do it?" she asked. "In accordance with the directions Christ gave his twelve disciples, when he called them together, and sent them forth to preach the gospel. 'When he had called unto him his twelve disciples, he gave them power against unclean spirits, to cast them out, and to heal

---

11   General Conference Bulletin, April 10, 1901, pp. 172–178.
12   Ibid., p. 176.
13   Ibid., pp. 181, 182.
14   General Conference Bulletin, April 9, 1901, p. 143.
15   General Conference Bulletin, April 17, 1901, pp. 282–284.
16   General Conference Bulletin, April 10, 1901, p. 184.

all manner of sickness, and all manner of disease.'

"I know that medical missionary work is the gospel, in practice, and, as the Lord has declared, is never, never to be separated from the gospel ministry."[17]

The delegates attempted to unify the medical branch with the church ministry by making five people from the Medical Missionary Association part of the twenty-five-member General Conference Committee. The resolution from the committee on organization read as follows: "That five of these members be chosen with special reference to their ability to foster and develop the true evangelical spirit in all departments of the work, to build up the ministry of the word, and to act as teachers of the gospel message in all parts of the world; and that they be relieved from any special business cares, that they may be free to devote themselves to this work."[18]

During the meetings Kellogg entertained the entire General Conference delegation with a dinner at the sanitarium. The meal was described as consisting of "the most toothsome delicacies, consisting of grains and vegetables exquisitely served, followed by delicious fruits and assorted nuts. Everybody seemed to engage in the task before him, as if he enjoyed it. And why should it not be so? It was a dinner fit for any potentate of earth. One remarked that he did not see why anyone, with such food in abundance, should desire to gorge himself with the flesh of a dead animal. All in hearing agreed that such a menu was far preferable to the old system of meat diet. It was indeed a pleasant occasion, and one to which many will doubtless look back to as an excellent demonstration of what a proper diet should consist."[19]

Nevertheless, historical tensions between Adventist medical and evangelistic workers apparently came up at the conference. It was reported that the brethren had openly talked about their differences and seemed to have discredited some false reports.

"After it was made plain that the evil rumors in circulation were without foundation, by one united, hearty amen, all agreed to drop all these things from their conversation, and, to do all in their power to correct the false impressions which have already gained a footing in the minds of brethren throughout the field.

"If this shall be done, suspicion will be allayed, dark hints of covert wrong will cease to be given, and even remote allusion to that which would create suspicion will soon become a thing of the past. Such a state of things is most earnestly desired by all the delegates, we believe, because most of them see that by such means alone can be brought about the unity of purpose and of effort necessary to carry the great truths of the third angel's message to a needy world. In this condition of things, the ministry will recognize the medical missionary work as an essential factor in evangelizing the world, preparatory to the Lord's return to claim his people. Not only will the medical branch be recognized, by the ministry, but it will be fostered and upheld in its laudable work. May God speed that day."[20]

---

17 General Conference Bulletin, April 12, 1901, pp. 203–205.
18 General Conference Bulletin, April 11, 1901, p. 1.
19 General Conference Bulletin, April 15, 1901, p. 1.
20 General Conference Bulletin, April 18, 1901, pp. 305, 306.

A Profile of John Harvey Kellogg:

A Ministry Without Ministers

John Harvey Kellogg was born on February 26, 1852, into a devout Adventist family. His father was prominent among the early Battle Creek Adventists, and his older half-brother, Merritt Kellogg, assisted J. N. Loughborough in opening up Adventist work in California after the Civil War.

When his mother died, Ellen White described her as "a noble woman, true as steel to principle, and I always highly respected her and loved her as a sincere devoted servant of Jesus Christ, as a tried friend, as one whom you knew was reliable under all and every circumstance."[1]

An obituary of his father, J. P. Kellogg, said he became an Adventist in 1852, the year John Harvey was born. He was active in the Advent movement until his death at the age of seventy-four in 1881. His first assignment was to manage tent operations in Michigan in 1856. He also served on the three-man publishing committee of the Review and Herald. He was one of the "corporatores" of the Review and Herald Publishing association organized in 1861, one of nine people to sign the articles of incorporation of the Western Heath Reform Institute in 1867, and one of its biggest subscribers to capital stock.

He opened up a broom shop and small store in Battle Creek, paying his son John Harvey $6 a week to work in it.

A combination of poor health and little emphasis on education among Seventh-day Adventists kept John Harvey out of school until he was nine years of age. But he quickly made up for lost time. From the money he earned in the family broom shop, he purchased a four-volume set of Farr's Ancient History, and he soon had a private library on shorthand, botany, astronomy, German, and grammar. He

---

1   Ellen G. White to John Harvey Kellogg, October 2, 1893, Ellen G. White Estate.

also owned a dictionary. Furthermore, he learned to play the piano, organ, and violin.

James White quickly recognized the ripening mental abilities of twelve-year-old John Harvey Kellogg and hired him at the Review. During the next four years, he rapidly advanced from errand and cleanup boy to typesetter, proofreader, and finally editorial consultant.

This job introduced him to the health principles Ellen White had seen in vision. The Review and Herald started publishing books and tracts on health, all of which young John Harvey Kellogg read avidly during the course of his work. He became converted to "health reform" principles to the point of spending one summer sleeping on newspapers for a mattress to correct a tendency toward round shoulders.

At the age of nineteen, he published his first article sketching the life of King Cyrus in the March 15, 1871, *The Youth's Instructor*. "We need more of that firmness and decision of character which young Cyrus had," he concluded. "We should serve God from principle, and should have that principle so firmly fixed in our hearts that circumstances cannot affect us. May the Lord give us courage to do right."

The next year he sketched a history of the Bible in that same magazine, saying we should "study it carefully, obey its precepts, and heed its warnings, that we may be prepared to realize the consummation of its promises."[2]

A few years later, in 1886, he wrote to Ellen White, "I most sincerely crave your prayers that God will give me grace and strength to bear my trials patiently and that the lessons which are set to me to learn may result in making me a purer, gentler, more patient and Christlike man. I do not doubt that every trial I have had has been absolutely necessary to keep me humble, and that I have had not one too many.… it has seemed to me a great many times that He did help me and uphold me in spite of my utter unworthiness. When the cloud has passed over, I am too prone to forget, and become so engrossed with my work that I lose my feeling of dependence upon the Lord and I wonder that the Lord has any forbearance with me."[3]

"I cannot thank you sufficiently for your kindness in writing me so many instructive and encouraging letters," Kellogg wrote to Ellen White in Australia in 1892. "Your letters always come like an inspiration to me, and give me hope and courage when I am sometimes so nearly crushed by cares and anxieties and perplexities, and so completely worn out with work and loss of sleep, that I feel almost as though life was not worth living."

Kellogg always held Ellen White in high regard, and he corresponded extensively with her, at least until the Seventh-day Adventist Church parted company with him. Yet he seemed to address her more as a person of influence, one of God's ordained leaders of the young Adventist movement, than a prophetess. He needed the support of the church and, thus, the endorsement of Ellen White to successfully operate his sanitarium and schools in Battle Creek. His many letters to her seem to be more of an attempt to promote his programs than to ask the will of the Lord.

---

2 *The Youth's Instructor*, May 1872, p. 1.

3 John Harvey Kellogg to Ellen G. White, December 6, 1886, Ellen G. White Estate.

The Beginnings of the Sanitarium

Of course, Kellogg had a lot to offer. The Battle Creek Sanitarium took off with him at the helm. In 1890 he wrote of a growing program with the possibility of a medical school. "We have concluded to raise the old part of the main building one story in addition to the new part on the north end. Our work is rapidly approaching completion.... We need the room very much indeed."[4]

The next year he estimated the "san," short for sanitarium, had 400 patients being educated in proper eating habits and a vegetarian lifestyle. "We are making constant headway in exalting our principles, and have nearly twenty young men and women who are thoroughly enlisted in the work and are committed to the strictest interpretation of the principles which the Sanitarium have represented for so many years.

"At a recent meeting of the General Conference Committee with our Board and the Medical Students, the Committee also endorsed our principles—vegetarian principles and all....

"When you return [from Australia] two years hence, I think I shall be able to report that meat scarcely appears upon the Sanitarium table at all."[5]

He clearly believed what Ellen White taught about diet and caring for the physical needs of patients. In 1892 he wrote, "We hope to go into the building next spring. The old main building of the Sanitarium is crowded full and we have had to provide room outside."[6]

"It is the principles which the Lord has given us, and which we are trying to carry out and promulgate here in the institution, which enables these doctors and nurses to combat disease more successfully than others, and I believe the principle is right that those who are received into the institution and given an opportunity to acquire a knowledge of these principles, should devote themselves to the interests of the cause and not to the building up of selfish individual enterprises."[7]

A few years later he reported, "Our work is going on beautifully. We are brim-full of patients. We have between twelve and thirteen hundred people now at the Sanitarium, in all the various departments. There is a great interest among the people to know our principles. We never had so many inquiries for light and truth."[8]

A number of years later, in September 1905, Kellogg wrote, "We have been having a great crowd of patients this summer. Almost without exception, they have seemed to be very eager to receive the truth which we have tried to present to them. The Lord has helped us in our efforts to take care of them. We have had a sufficient number of good helpers to do them justice, so that I trust the influence of the work has been better than last year."[9]

Speaking about Ellen White's book *Steps to Christ*, Kellogg seemed to praise her more as an outstanding Christian author rather than as a prophetess under divine inspiration.

---

4   Ibid., June 4, 1890.
5   Ibid., August 23, 1891.
6   Ibid., September 1892.
7   Ibid., September 9, 1892.
8   Ibid., August 22, 1897.
9   Ibid., September 10, 1905.

"I have been reading your little book, "Steps to Christ," one of the first copies of which I obtained from the publishers, and am delighted with it. I had previously read some works of Anna Whitehall Smith, and others, which contained many good thoughts, but your method of treating the subject is certainly masterly."[10]

But within this letter he hinted at an area of disagreement he would eventually have with Ellen White in approaching the general public in a non-sectarian way. "I am glad the book is published by an outside publishing house, as this will bring it into the hands of a large number of people, and will be the best kind of an introduction for you and your other books."[11]

Later that same year he informed Ellen White that he was sharing the book with others. "For several weeks I had been having our helpers meet every Sunday evening and have been reading to them the special testimonies which you have sent us from time to time…. The truths presented in your little work "Steps to Christ," seem to have taken a fast hold of a large proportion of our helpers here. I do not believe there is another institution among us, not excepting our schools, where so many persons possessed of a real missionary spirit can be found together."[12]

His opinion of her as an authority figure showed in the form of an invitation to Ellen White to stay at his home while attending the 1900 General Conference session in Battle Creek. "I am anxious to lose no opportunity to show our people and the public that I hold you in the highest esteem and respect and have the most complete confidence in you."[13]

Nonsectarian View

When the sanitarium and medical missionary boards voted to start a medical school in 1895, with training at Battle Creek and Chicago, he agreed with Ellen White on the danger of sending Adventist students to state medical schools. "The very evils you speak of I see clearly developing among our students at Ann Arbor."[14]

Less than one month after his letter to Ellen White regarding the dangers of a secular education, he reported incorporating the Medical College on June 13, 1895. "We hope to have it in operation by next fall, so we shall have to send no more students away to Ann Arbor, or other medical schools—at any rate not until they have had a good groundwork of principles laid."[15]

In spite of his concern for the well-being of the students and their exposure to the world, Kellogg was hesitant to link medical missionary work with the church. This was evident in his medical missionary approach to the South. It included self-supporting sale of health foods, circulation of *Good*

---

10   Ibid., February 10, 1892.
11   Ibid.
12   Ibid., October 3, 1892.
13   Ibid., March 3, 1901.
14   Ibid., May 26, 1895.
15   Ibid., June 13, 1895.

Health magazine, and nursing work for the rich and poor, but there was no mention of the church.[16] He believed that medical missionary work should be nonsectarian.[17]

This nonsectarian view was further expressed when he declined the position as medical secretary of the General Conference in 1897. In a letter to Ellen White, he wrote, "I did not think it would be well for the medical missionary work to go before the public as being under the supervision of a church organization like the General Conference, but that it would be better for it to go before the world as a Christian and gospel work without sectarian trammels… I say our people have shown so little interest in the true work which we ought to have been carrying forward, and have been so much given to acrimonious discussion, etc., that a tremendous prejudice has been stirred up, so that people are afraid of anything that looks like church work on the part of Seventh-day Adventists.

"The medical missionary work is well calculated to break down this prejudice and open the way for the gospel, which brings along with it the Sabbath and all the rest of our precious truths," he continued. "I think it would be much better, on this account as well as on other accounts, that our medical missionary work should be carried forward by a separate and distinct organization, just as the religious liberty work is, and just as our sanitariums are, so that we could say, This work is not denominational work, but it is a work undertaken for God and humanity."[18]

> "Genuine medical missionary work is in no case to become divorced from the gospel ministry.…"

He accordingly organized the International Medical Missionary and Benevolent Association to work in Chicago and the South and act in harmony with the Foreign Mission Board.[19] In 1901 he reported that it employed 2,400 persons and had a net financial worth of more than $2 million.[20]

Based on this philosophy, in 1897 he renewed the charter of the Battle Creek Sanitarium by officially declaring it nonsectarian and tax exempt, meaning its income could be spent only in the state of Michigan.

Ellen White completely disagreed with this viewpoint. "Never, never should a sanitarium be established to become an interest independent of the church," she wrote to him in 1899. "Genuine medical missionary work is in no case to become divorced from the gospel ministry. The cross is the center of all religious institutions. These institutions are to be under the control of the Spirit of God, and no one man is to be the sole head in these institutions. The divine mind has men for every place."[21]

---

16   Ibid., May 26, 1895.
17   Ibid., August 23, 1891.
18   Ibid., May 4, 1897.
19   Ibid.
20   John Harvey Kellogg to students of the American Medical Missionary College, September 5, 1901, Ellen G. White Estate.
21   Ellen G. White to John Harvey Kellogg, December 12, 1899, Ellen G. White Estate.

Mrs. White felt that some of the profits from the thriving Battle Creek Sanitarium should help establish Adventist medical institutions in less-privileged places such as Australia. Kellogg responded by raising $5,000 in personal donations to help the struggling new Adventist hospital in Sydney.[22]

His attempt to distance the medical missionary work from the Seventh-day Adventist Church had begun years before. In 1892 a World's Fair opened in Chicago, and Kellogg wanted to establish a presence there by advertising the Battle Creek Sanitarium. His ultimate goal was to follow it up with a mission to the poor and outcast of that city.

"After the fair is over, if we conclude that it is best to do so, we can continue our headquarters for missionary work in Chicago," he wrote to Willie White in Australia.

He mentioned wanting to continue the work of a Colonel Clark, a former patient of his at the sanitarium, who had started the Pacific Garden Mission in "one of the most needy portions of the city."

"If we ever start in Chicago, we must start in such a place and in such a manner as to convince the world that our purpose is to do good and not simply to proselyte," he wrote. "Our intense sectarianism has been the cause of creating more enemies to our work than the doctrines which are peculiar to our faith. I am more and more convinced all the time that the sarcastic and savage manner in which Jones and Waggoner, and others whose names I might mention, have been in the habit of treating our opponents, has been laying up for us a tremendous retribution, which, when it comes, we shall call persecution for righteousness sake, but it will be, as a matter of fact, only just punishment for our lack of charity, Christian meekness and kindliness.…

"I am satisfied that the work here in the Sanitarium has been injured a good deal by too much sectarian effort and still more by a lack of activity in Gospel missionary work," he added.[23]

Ellen White initially approved of the work in Chicago, but she warned him against confining it to the lower classes. "Brother Kellogg, the Lord calls for a halt, while you sit down and count the cost, to see whether you will be able to finish the building which you have begun. My brother, you are in danger. You are making many plans that you can never carry through. In your effort to embrace so much in the rescue work, you are in danger of divorcing yourself from the leading and most urgent features of the last gospel message."

She went on to discuss the need for ministers to be involved in the medical work. "There must be camp meetings held to reach all classes, and at every place where these camp meetings are held, a home should be established where educated workers can teach all classes of learners how to work in medical missionary lines in connection with the Bible workers. All are to be taught how to carry the work to towns and cities that have not yet heard the message. Thus the light of truth will shine forth in many places. Meeting-houses must be built and humble buildings hired or erected where treatment can be given to the sick. By this means the work of the gospel and the medical missionary work will be bound together."[24]

---

22   Arthur L. White, *The Australian Years, 1891-1900*, vol. 4, p. 398.
23   John Harvey Kellogg to Willie C. White, June 30, 1892, Ellen G. White Estate.
24   Ellen G. White to John Harvey Kellogg, August 29, 1899, Ellen G. White Estate.

She pointed out that the medical work was to be administered to all classes of people, not just the poor as Kellogg seemed inclined to focus on. Furthermore, she counseled him in the importance of coupling the medical work with preaching the gospel.

His approach to city evangelism seemed counterproductive to her. "I saw the large work established by you in Chicago, and the money that was invested," she wrote. "There was presented before me a long roll of paper, having upon it figures of a startling character, while in large letters was inscribed, 'Consumers, but not producers.' The figures showed the amount of God's money that had been invested in that enterprise in Chicago, and the results to the work all over the world. The representation was most disheartening..."[25]

She saw the work of ministers as being just as important as that of Kellogg as a physician. "Our work in camp meetings brings us in touch with all nationalities and all classes, rich and poor, high and low; and it brings us in connection with the sick and suffering. These camp meetings should be regarded as verily God's instrumentalities as are the sanitariums. Their work is essential."[26]

She felt that confining his Chicago work mostly to the lower classes would dilute the third angel's message. "The light came to me clear and distinct that the medical missionary work was absorbing too much, while a more definite work in special lines was being neglected, that you were gather into your arms a class of work that is never ending, which was eclipsing the work that needs to be done in every city—the proclamation of the coming of Christ. The Third Angel's Message was being blanketed and you were not altogether straight on these things."[27]

A general humanitarian work seemed to satisfy him. "The development of our work goes on in a wonderfully interesting way," he wrote concerning it in October 1897.

Prominent people taking a serious interest in the Chicago mission included the president of Northwestern University, "the greatest Methodist University in the world," and the editor of the Northwestern Christian Advocate, "one of the leading Methodist papers."[28]

He wrote of a missionary nurse in Chicago, working among "the very lowest class of people where no other nurses have ever been before," which attracted the attention of a prominent banker who offered to support her while he was alive and who made provision for her should he die. "There is a demand for this kind of work in every large city in the United States," he concluded in the same letter.[29]

In 1898 he moved his Chicago enterprise to State Street and named it the Life Boat Mission. "It is in a better locality than our old mission ... and will reach a better crowd," he wrote to Ellen White.[30]

In conjunction with starting the mission in Chicago, Kellogg expressed his deep desire to work for the poor in a letter to Ellen White dated August 5, 1895. "Our institution pretends to be a philanthropic

---

25 Ellen G. White, *Manuscript Releases*, vol. 4, p. 138.
26 Ibid., p. 140.
27 Ellen G. White to John Harvey Kellogg, March 24, 1899, Ellen G. White Estate.
28 John Harvey Kellogg to Ellen G. White, October 25, 1897, Ellen G. White Estate.
29 Ibid., December 22, 1892.
30 Ibid., April 14, 1898.

establishment, but we are not doing for the poor a tenth part of what we ought to do. It seems to me that we ought to have forty or fifty beds, where worthy poor people could receive the best advantages which medical science can afford, free of charge."[31]

Then on December 6, 1886, "My highest ambition in this world is to get the Sanitarium upon such a footing that it will be able to support 75 or 100 free beds for the worthy poor." He pledged $5,000 for such a building and reported an average of 265 patients during the winter despite serious attempts from competitors to lure them away.

The Religious Aspect of Kellogg's Work

Although he wanted the sanitarium to be nonsectarian, religion was an important part of his program. In 1886 he wrote about the 180 patients who were at the sanitarium at the time. "The thing I now desire most of all is that we may be in a position in which the Lord can bless us, and our work to the saving of souls. We have a very intelligent class of patients here, and there is a very remarkable interest in our views. We keep a large rack full of tracts near the entrance, which requires daily filling, as patients send so many away to their friends."[32]

The next month, March 1886, he wrote, "I am glad to report to you a state of prosperity in all departments of our work which is quite unprecedented. We have at the present time something more than 250 patients, more than a hundred more than ever before at this season of the year, and a class of patients of whom any institution might be proud."[33]

In another letter he commented, "Our religious interest is good, I think, and there is much interest among the patients. We are having a series of denominational lectures given in the gymnasium every Friday evening....

"We are still keeping up our morning meetings, and with a better attendance and interest than at any previous time. I think that nearly every helper who can do so attends every morning. In addition we have been having for two weeks a manager's prayer meeting at noon, at which all in charge of the different departments are present, and the physicians. I do think that the Lord is blessing us some in opening our eyes to the magnitude of our work, the obligations and responsibilities which are connected with it especially as regards the spiritual welfare of those who come here. We are very full of patients, and more coming, although we have hardly a room left in our large building."[34]

A few years later he reported, "I am glad to report a constant growth in a missionary spirit in our institution. Our patients feel the influence of the good spirit which prevails and within a few weeks five of our leading patients have embraced the truth and several others are upon the point of doing so....

"Our people, it seems to me, have made a great mistake in looking down upon themselves as being inferior to the rest of the world, as that they could not be expected to amount to much anyway. With

---

31 Ibid., August 5, 1895.
32 Ibid., February 7, 1886.
33 Ibid., March 20, 1886.
34 Ibid., October 15, 1886.

the light which the Lord has given us and the opportunities before us we ought to be in the very front ranks in progress in everything, and it is a great shame and discredit to us that we are not."[35]

In 1897 he reported to Ellen White that they had twelve conversions in Battle Creek, all but one among them sanitarium patients, and more than a hundred conversions in Chicago during a two-week period, one of whom was a fallen evangelist. Kellogg described him as "ready to scrub floors, whitewash walls, run errands, and do anything." He and his wife later became "thoroughly established in the truth."[36]

The positive reports from Chicago continued. "Our work in Chicago is being greatly blessed at the present time. We have evening meetings every night, and one night last week there were four very striking conversions. We have one or two apparently very genuine conversions every night, and often more…

"I wish we had such as mission in every city in the land. We do not give all our attention to the poor or the degraded classes. We have three or four workers connected with our mission there; our doctors attend to the wounds and diseases of the suffering ones no matter how bad they are, or how miserable they are, at certain hours every day, then the rest of the time is devoted to the wealthy. The fact that we are doing something for these neglected classes makes friends with the rich. Our work among this class has grown to such an extent that the building we at first occupied—formerly the old Chicago Mission building, which you have often visited, I believe—at 28 College Place, has long been filled to overflowing. We have had to hire another building, in which we store away nearly as many persons, and I have this week hired still another building 120 feet in length, two stories in height."[37]

A few weeks later he described the work in Chicago as "getting along splendidly. I brought home with me last week a deed for $10,000 worth of fine property which has been given by Mr. Kimball, an outsider, for the Medical College. We shall be able to raise the whole $100,000 I am sure without making drafts on our people." He also reported "a good spirit among the students of the Medical College. Prof. Prescott is giving them studies each week which I am sure they appreciate. I wish all our people would receive and appreciate the truths which Prof. Prescott and Dr. Waggoner are presenting on the subject of life."[38]

He also reported a booming food business generating $1,000 a month and possibilities of earning four times that.[39]

"I spent last Sunday in Chicago as usual, had a most interesting time," he wrote to her in 1896. "I spoke forty-five minutes in one of the fashionable churches with a large audience, they gave the closest attention and seemed deeply touched as I told them of the situation of the poor men for whom we are working, and how the gospel saved them from their miserable condition … Donations are almost daily

---

35   Ibid., December 22, 1892.
36   Ibid., November 24, 1897.
37   Ibid., April 18, 1895.
38   Ibid., June 1895.
39   Ibid., April 18, 1895.

coming in from wealthy people in Chicago and elsewhere to help along the work."[40]

None could deny his impact. He reported seeing 180 to 200 people every night in Chicago in 1896, and he had plans to start a similar work in an old Battle Creek saloon.[41]

"We are trying to get all our workers into such a state of mind that the week-day work, as well as the Sabbath-day work, will seem a real religious service from morning to night," he wrote concerning his Chicago work in 1897.[42]

"Not a week passes that we do not have conversions," he wrote to Ellen White in 1897. "Recently twelve persons were converted in our food department, where about sixty are employed."[43]

Kellogg's Rising Fame

His influence outside of the Adventist Church became more prominent as the years went by. A lecture tour took him to Cleveland, Toronto, Chicago, and Louisville.[44] In addition, he became involved in other interdenominational work. He reported supporting a Methodist preacher in India and a Baptist preacher somewhere else, paying half the expenses for ten boys in a school operated by a Bishop Thoburn and subsidizing two free beds for patients in the Seventh-day Baptist Hospital in Shanghai.[45]

On the fifth anniversary of his Chicago mission, he described it as "going on gloriously." During this time, similar missions started in cities like Brooklyn, Milwaukee, St . Louis, Omaha, Kansas City, Lincoln, Denver, Portland, Oregon, San Francisco, Salt Lake City, and other metropolitan areas. A few years later he noticed cooperation in England, somewhat in Scandinavia, and "quite thoroughly in Germany."[46]

A big-time soul winning success story came from all of the missionary work he was involved in. In a letter written November 28, 1898, he reported to Ellen White of a great interest among Brooklyn ministers in the New York Medical Mission. He planned to feed them a vegetarian lunch at an association meeting. One of their most prominent members, Dr. Isaac Funk, cofounder of the Funk & Wagnalls publishing company, had become a "staunch vegetarian." His daughter, Lida Funk Scott, had come to the Battle Creek Sanitarium for surgery a few weeks before. "Last week, to my surprise, she stopped me in the hall, telling me that by her own investigation, she had become a Sabbath-keeper. She expects to be baptized next Sabbath."

Scott, then living in Montclair, New Jersey, became an active Seventh-day Adventist in the Newark Church. She remained a believer in Ellen White and, after 1914, became a disciple of Edward A. Sutherland and Percy Magan. Unlike their friend Kellogg, they encouraged their people to go out

---

40   Ibid., January 4, 1896.
41   Ibid., December 30, 1896.
42   Ibid., January 24, 1897.
43   Ibid., October 1, 1897.
44   Ibid., October 25, 1897.
45   Ibid., May 26, 1895.
46   Ibid., February 15, 1900.

from the Madison, Tennessee, base and start small schools and sanitariums all over the South. She dedicated her personal fortune to extending the work of Madison and also made her home there. At the encouragement of Sutherland, she gave large sums of money to develop the Los Angeles campus of the struggling College of Medical Evangelists because of their great need of physicians. She founded the Layman Foundation in 1924, which remained active for many years after her death in 1945.

When Kellogg was not traveling or speaking, he worked an eighteen-hour day seeing patients, performing sometimes back-to-back surgeries, editing a health magazine, and writing books and articles at night. In a November 4, 1892, letter he wrote to Ellen White about his work establishing a nurse's training school, a health and temperance course, and a medical course to train physicians.

Kellogg's growing reputation and the fame and fortune of his successful medical practice and the elevated position of Battle Creek on the national stage beg the question as to whether he saw the importance of Ellen White's counsel. His correspondence seems to indicate an agreement with her message itself rather than confidence in its source as direct revelations from heaven. He sent his most revealing letter to Willie White, son and top aide of Ellen White, in 1895 protesting the apathy of leading Adventists, perhaps including Willie himself, to vegetarianism.

> "I try to live out health principles ... because they were right and true in themselves...."

"I cannot understand why there is such slowness to follow the light the Lord has given us upon this point and especially why you whose relations are so close to the source of light to our people—should have been so slow upon these points during all these years, not only as regards the conducting of the work but as regards the living out of the principles themselves. I try to live out health principles not because your mother's teachings have advocated them, but because they were right and true in themselves, and my faith in your mother's teachings has been based on my belief in the fundamental correctness of the principles which she teaches rather than upon any particular disposition to trust in the supernatural."[47]

He wrote essentially the same thing to Ellen White in 1905. "I have received, doubtless through your kind suggestion, a copy of your new book, 'Ministry of Healing'. It is indeed a beautiful volume, and I have greatly enjoyed perusing it. It will shed a flood of light and truth wherever it is received and read. I am heartily in accord with every principle expressed in it; and so far as I know, speaking for myself and my colleagues, we are not, here at the Sanitarium, at the present time at least, teaching anything which is not thoroughly in harmony with the teachings of your book; at least, we are not consciously doing so. Anything which I have taught which is not in harmony with this work, I would gladly retract. I have no desire or purpose to teach any doctrine in relation to life and duty which could be reasonably considered in antagonism to the sound and beautiful truths which you have set forth in 'Ministry of Healing.'"[48]

---

47   John Harvey Kellogg to Willie C. White, August 7, 1895, Ellen G. White Estate.
48   John Harvey Kellogg to Ellen G. White, September 10, 1905, Ellen G. White Estate.

In 1879 he described her as being "the most instructive and interesting lady temperance lecturer who has appeared before the public."[49]

To him, what she said and wrote made sense and was enough to make him a celebrity. He always regarded himself as a friend and major beneficiary of Ellen White; she and her husband, James, encouraged him to go to medical school as a young man. Although he owed much of his fame and fortune to Ellen White, there runs through his correspondence and relationship with her a strain of reservation. He kept her up to date on what he was doing, especially during the years she lived in Australia, but that did not keep him from having his own ideas on how to do things. During the struggling early years of Adventism, Kellogg seemed to personify success. He was a rising star, a brilliant young man attracting attention, bringing in money, performing surgeries, founding cereal companies, writing books, giving lectures, helping start a temperance society, and changing lifestyles.

Ellen White herself called him "the greatest physician in the world."[50]

An example of his skills and workload was documented in a letter written to her in 1892. "Week before last one operation consisted in removing an enormous kidney as large as a person's head, inside of which I found a stone as large as a lemon. The patient made a good recovery but it gave me great anxiety for several days and nights. I have three patients in the ward for whom I performed the operation of removing the womb and both ovaries to which was connected an enormous tumor in each case. I have two more of this sort tomorrow besides other cases. In the last three years I have had nearly 350 cases in which the abdomen was opened. More than 200 of these were cases of a most serious character—tumors, abscesses, etc., and have given me great mental anxiety and care in looking after them."[51]

In a letter dated April 18, 1895, Kellogg reported to Ellen White, "I had a succession of 175 cases without a death. Ten of these were cases in which the entire womb and both ovaries were removed. Of 70 cases of ovarian tumors which I have removed, some of them very large, only one patient died. In 55 cases of large tumors of the womb, there was one death. In 319 cases, including those mentioned, there were only 3 deaths. These records are far ahead of the best records which have ever been made by the most famous surgeons in the world. I attribute the success not to my own skill (although I endeavor to do my best in every case) but to the hygienic care of the patients before and after operation."

Ellen White tried to put his success into perspective. "Who has been by your side as you have performed these critical operations? Who has kept you calm and self-possessed in the crisis, giving you quick, sharp discernment, clear eyesight, steady nerves, and skillful precision? The Lord Jesus has sent His angel to your side to tell you what to do. A hand has been laid upon your hand. Jesus, and not you, has guided the movements of your instrument. At times you have realized this, and a wonderful calmness has come over you. You dared not hurry, and yet you worked rapidly, knowing that there was not a moment to lose. The Lord has greatly blessed you.... As you looked to God in your critical operations,

---

49 *The Signs of the Times*, July 3, 1879, p. 205.
50 Ellen G. White to John Harvey Kellogg, December 10, 1899, Ellen G. White Estate.
51 John Harvey Kellogg to Ellen G. White, September 1892, Ellen G. White Estate.

angels of God were standing by your side, and their hands were seen as your hand performing the work with an accuracy that made the beholders surprised" (*Selected Messages*, book 2, p. 285).

Kellogg was aware of this. "When in deep trouble and perplexity I have often renewed this vow [to give all glory for success to God]. Many times when … nothing but a miracle could save my patient, I have for an instant closed my eyes and begged God for skill and wisdom to save the life of the mother of innocent little ones, and I have had evidence that God has heard my prayer. I have always promised God I would give him all the glory, and I have tried to do so."[52]

In spite of his success, in a letter to Ellen White, Kellogg admitted that he did not relish his job as a surgeon. "It is now a little more than twenty years since I started out in the study of medicine, against my will. The first ten years I rebelled against my lot as I found surgical work, the most loathsome thing connected with medicine … It is a perfect horror to me to have to cut into human beings, but there is such wide opportunities opening up before the physician outside of surgery and the treatment of loathsome maladies that I really enjoy my work and only desire abundance of strength and vigor to do it."[53]

When Kellogg took charge of the struggling sanitarium in Battle Creek upon finishing medical school in New York, he quickly energized the place. "The family at the Sanitarium now numbers ninety-nine, besides twenty-five who just come in for treatment; and new patients are arriving every few day," wrote James White. "Dr. J. H. Kellogg has the entire confidence of the patients, by whom he is justly held in high esteem."[54]

That same year in the October 4 issue of *The Advent Review and Sabbath Herald*, James White reported the formation of a committee to change the name of the sanitarium. Kellogg was a member of the committee that came up with Battle Creek Sanitarium. By the next year, they announced the formation of a school of hygiene. Then, in addressing the General Conference of 1878, Mr. White referred to the sanitarium "as an institution of no small importance." He boasted of a strong medical staff with John Harvey Kellogg, M.D., at the head, assisted by Miss Lindsay, M.D., and Miss Lamson, M.D. "These are all Christians, Seventh-day Adventists, looking for the coming of the Son of man in the clouds of heaven."[55]

Later in 1878 the board borrowed $25,000 to enlarge the facilities. The new building, upon completion, could accommodate 300 patients, and already had a clientele of 120 and growing.

"The reputation of this institution is such abroad, and especially in this city and State, and the people have such confidence in the integrity of S. D. Adventists, that three hundred can be gathered here as well as one hundred," Mr. White wrote in a report in June 13, 1878.[56]

An ad in the June 3, 1880, *Advent Review and Sabbath Herald* described the "medical and surgical sanitarium" as a "great sanitarium of the west," boasting "more than 4,000 patients successfully treated.

---

52 Ibid., June 20, 1896.
53 Ibid., January 24, 1893.
54 *Advent Review and Sabbath Herald*, June 7, 1877, p. 184.
55 J*Advent Review and Sabbath Herald*, March 14, 1878, p. 1.
56 *The Advent Review and Sabbath Herald*, June 13, 1878, p. 188.

The erection of new buildings and the addition of the most approved remedial appliances known to the profession, have made it The Most Complete Institution of the Kind in America."

Kellogg and the sanitarium were an asset to an unpopular religious group still finding its footing. During his first year on the job, Kellogg went to the centennial exposition in Philadelphia and handed out Adventist literature.

Denominational Support and Opposition

We will never know if his success caused jealousy among the brethren, but some people at the seventeenth annual session of the General Conference in October 1878 questioned his theology, which was perhaps a foretaste of what lay ahead. "The impression has gone out from some unknown cause that J. H. Kellogg, M.D., holds infidel sentiments, which does him great injustice, and also endangers his influence as physician-in-chief of the Sanitarium," according to a report.[57]

The conference then gave him an opportunity to state his views. "In accordance with the foregoing resolution, Dr. Kellogg gave, before a large audience, October 6, an able address on the harmony of science and the Bible, for which the congregation tendered him a vote of thanks."[58]

He then published his address in a book titled *The Soul and the Resurrection* "showing the Harmony of Science and the Bible on the Nature of the Soul and the Doctrine of the Resurrection," according to an advertisement in a number of issues of *The Advent Review and Sabbath Herald* in 1879. "This work is the outgrowth of an address delivered by request before the S. D. A General Conference held in October, 1878."

"We have read and re-read the book with extreme delight; and can recommend it without the least degree of hesitation as a work eminently calculated to free skeptical thinking minds from popular objections against the blessed Bible," wrote James White. "The first edition is small, and will be very soon exhausted."[59]

"We think it superior to any work upon that subject that we have ever examined," wrote S. N. Haskell. "It should be placed in the hands of the youth everywhere.... The subject is scientifically discussed, and made plain to the commonest reader. Wherever the book is read and heeded it will stay the tide of evil which is overflowing the land."[60]

J. N. Andrews, writing from Basel, Switzerland, in May 1878, also highly recommended it. "Dr. Zimple of Puteoli, Italy, a physician of eminent ability and well learned in science, said to me at his residence last September, 'This book by Dr. Kellogg is one of the most remarkable books that was ever written.'"[61]

He also started publishing *Good Health* magazine and helped organize the American Health and Temperance Association.

---

57   General Conference Bulletin, October 4, 1878, p. 127.
58   Ibid.
59   *Advent Review and Sabbath Herald,* February 27, 1879, p. 72.
60   *Advent Review and Sabbath Herald,* May 10, 1877, p. 152.
61   *Advent Review and Sabbath Herald,* May 30, 1878, p. 176.

An ad for *Good Health*, listing J. H. Kellogg as editor, boasted that it had "the largest circulation of any health journal in America and the publishers are determined, not only to maintain the high position already attained, but to greatly increase its circulation the coming year, and thus enlarge its field of usefulness."[62]

"Persons often speak of Dr. Kellogg as one whom God has especially called, and is using in his service," wrote Ellen White in the March 25, 1880, issue of *Advent Review and Sabbath Herald*. "But while we believe that he is a man of God, we believe that the Lord did not accept him to the exclusion of others. He has met the difficulties of his situation, and mastered them. He has improved his time to increase his talents, and God has accepted his labors."

Unfortunately, Kellogg's workaholic ways, along with those of J. N. Andrews and James White, concerned Ellen White. "I am much obliged for your solicitude for my health," he wrote to her on January 17, 1877. "You say 'Do not work nights.' I cannot help it. I work every day until I fall asleep in my chair from exhaustion. I promise to reform and the next night, work till 3 a.m. I feel bad about it. I am afraid my health will fail. But work presses, and if neglected, something or someone suffers."

His non-stop work habits apparently became such an issue that a special meeting of the General Conference Committee held in the home of James White on July 2, 1878, passed a resolution recommending that young Kellogg have periods of rest lasting several weeks three or four times a year.

"In our opinion, he is sinning against God and himself, and committing a wrong against the supporters and patrons of the Sanitarium in depriving himself of less than eight hours in bed in every twenty four, whether able to sleep or not," the resolution read.

Other recommendations included his being accessible at all hours of the day, though not allowing anyone into his room or office without permission, and sharing responsibilities with less experienced physicians.

"That we, the General Conference Committee, who have the oversight of the entire work, feel that it is our duty to control this matter, if at any time we shall see Dr. Kellogg violating the laws of health and life, and thus endangering the reputation and financial condition of the Sanitarium, which would result in bringing trial upon our people."

Perhaps this was a first salvo in a long power struggle to come. Ten years later, Kellogg was obviously still working a lot and had not heeded the church's counsel to slow down, because Ellen White wrote to him on February 23, 1887, saying, "You are living two years in one, and I utter my protest against that."

In 1892 he wrote that he started his day at 5 a.m. with a knock on his door by one of his stenographers. "After a few hours work on letters, papers, lectures, and editing our three journals, the Medical Missionary for our own people, Good Health for the world at large, and Modern Medicine for the doctors, I eat a little fruit and a cracker or two and take a little water gruel, and run over to the Sanitarium to lecture." After an hour's lecture, he saw patients in his office until 6 p.m., and went home for dinner.

---

62 *Advent Review and Sabbath Herald*, January 29, 1880, p. 79.

He would then see patients till 10 or 11 p.m. and read new medical books and journals. "I am seldom in bed before midnight and consider myself fortunate if before 1 o'clock in the morning."[63]

The whole enterprise seemed to revolve around him, a situation Ellen White opposed, but he had his reasons. "The doctors are familiar with the medical part, the managers know something about the business part, others know something of the literary part, but there is not one who follows me about through it all."[64]

Kellogg himself agreed with Ellen White on the issue of his heavy workload. On August 5, 1885, he wrote to her: "I see a great many mistakes that I have made and hope in many ways to do much better work than I have done, but there have been many weeks—I may say months—that I have had to work with such fearful physical odds against me, in the condition of my brain and nerves worn out with anxiety, that every day was a horror and a terror, and I plunged into my work every morning with sheer desperation, determined to struggle through it in some way, although so perplexed that everything seemed in a whirl."

A few years later, he further lamented as to his workload and the lack of rest. "I have to stay at home constantly—have had in the 20 years which I have been connected with the work here, only two brief vacations, when I went to Europe, and on both of these occasions I worked incessantly while I was gone, so I have actually had no vacation at all for 20 years … Sometimes I have had as high as six cases a day in which I have had to open the abdomen, to remove tumors or other products of disease, and in these cases everything depends upon incessant vigilance. I have had no one to whom even the after-care of these patients could be trusted."[65]

In 1899 he wrote he had sometimes worked "forty hours at a stretch without a minutes rest, and after five or six hours sleep was able to go into a long pull of twenty hours or more."[66]

Ellen White counseled him to share the responsibility of the work with others. "You must never take the position that because you have an experience in your calling and practice that others have not, everyone must meet your exact measurements in all particulars before you can take them by your side and teach them all you know yourself, … "[67]

In addition to wanting him to share his knowledge with less experienced physicians, Ellen White also wanted him to work with the ministers. "When you become one with your brethren, as is represented in the seventeenth chapter of John, you may expect the love and power of God to flow in rich currents into your soul. The work of God is not divided; it is one, and if there is any separation between the medical missionary work and the ministry, it will be because the Holy Spirit is not working upon hearts."[68]

---

63   John Harvey Kellogg to Ellen G. White, September 1892, Ellen G. White Estate.
64   Ibid.
65   Ibid., March 20, 1895.
66   Ibid., November 12, 1899.
67   Ellen G. White, *Manuscript Releases*, vol. 11, pp. 300, 301.
68   Ellen G. White, *Manuscript Releases*, vol. 5, p. 133.

"Our physicians are to unite with the work of the ministry of the gospel," she wrote in another letter that same year. "Souls are to be saved, that the name of God may be magnified, and the physician is not to feel when brought in contact with the higher classes of society that he must hide the peculiar characteristics which sanctification through the truth give him."[69]

His correspondence throughout the years revealed constant challenges as a result of opposition from ministers. In his letters he would complain of attacks from some people in the church who he felt should have been his friends.

"The real foundation of all our perplexities here is the fact that our people have not regarded the principles which were upheld here at the Sanitarium, and regarded the work as a branch of the cause," he wrote to Ellen White in 1891. "Our doctors have seen that members of the General Conference Committee, and other leading men, did not regard the principles being upheld here, in harmony with the views of the founders of the institution, and the principles laid down in your writings in the Testimonies, and elsewhere, consequently they have not attached much importance to these things, and my appeals in the matter have been looked upon as a sort of fanatical zeal. Eld. Butler pronounced me an extremist before the whole General Conference only three or four years ago; our young doctors heard what he said and knew perfectly well that I had not his support nor the support of others in my work. This has led them to think that the so-called principles of the Sanitarium were simply my notions, and of little account, and not heaven-given principles to be regarded sacredly and earnestly as belonging to the great body of truth which the Lord is giving to the world in these last days through the Third Angel's message. As a consequence of this erroneous way of looking at things, they have felt justified in regarding their relation to the Sanitarium as a mere business one rather than considering it as a great missionary effort in which they were honored in having a part."[70]

He complained that the leading ministers thought medical missionary work useless unless it brought in more church members. "I have been perplexed to understand some of the teachings of Elder Jones, Prof. Prescott, and Dr. Waggoner, as they seem to give the people a basis for such ideas, and especially the fact that they have shown no interest in the Orphan Home work nor any of our medical missionary and benevolent enterprises has been an apparent evidence that they do not consider the sort of work in which I have been engaged, and which has, in fact, occupied my whole life since I was a boy, of any especial value or importance."[71]

He complained of a fake healing to Willie White, saying the ministers had told two of his patients to abandon the use of remedies and just have faith. Two people died as a result.[72] A. T. Jones and W. W. Prescott clashed with him on the issue.

In this incident, he spoke of Ellen White as being a fellow believer of his. "You must not think from what I have written that I do not believe in faith," he continued. "I base my belief on this subject on

---

69   Ibid., p. 134.
70   John Harvey Kellogg to Ellen G. White, October 2, 1891, Ellen G. White Estate.
71   Ibid., March 21, 1893.
72   John Harvey Kellogg to Willie C. White, January 27, 1892, Ellen G. White Estate.

what your mother has written in the Testimonies, and elsewhere, which commends itself to my good sense, and seems to me to agree with the Bible."[73]

His opinion of Ellen White showed in another letter regarding the matter: "It seems to me your petition will commend itself to the good sense and good judgment of all thinking people. But it is very different from the doctrine which has been taught by some of our brethren for the last few months."[74]

"The Lord showed us many years ago that our health and temperance work was to be an entering wedge," he wrote to Willie White in 1895.[75]

He reported some indications of progress in working with the brethren, such as in 1892 when the General Conference Committee decided to invite a physician to affiliate with each Adventist school in places like Lincoln, Nebraska; Healdsburg, California; Walla Walla, Washington; and South Lancaster, Massachusetts.

"This medical work will doubtless, in some instances at least, grow into a Sanitarium in connection with each of our particular schools."[76] In that same letter to J. D. Hare, Kellogg seemed pleased with the role of the General Conference. "The General Conference Committee are taking hold of the medical missionary work in good earnest, and are giving it every reasonable encouragement."[77]

However, just five days later he wrote to Willie White and seemed to complain about the church's leadership, commenting that their "actions have said louder than words could say that the principles taught in your mother's writings are of too little consequence to receive serious attention. This fact has been an almost insurmountable barrier to the progress of our work and to the maintenance of a correct standard here in the Sanitarium."[78]

He added he had found people at four camp meetings he had attended interested in health principles "but it has been my constant experience until this time that while the people were ready to receive the truth and to act, the ministers have stood squarely in the way either by their indifference or by active opposition."[79]

He wrote of "our leading brethren, toward our work here at the Sanitarium, ignoring it almost entirely for years at a time."[80] Kellogg regarded some conference presidents as being "'little popes' ... a man gets impressed with his own importance, thinks the Lord is leading him particularly and gets to be a regular tyrant because he thinks himself consecrated."[81]

"Some of them [conference presidents] cannot see any duty in encouraging anything but

---

73 Ibid.
74 John Harvey Kellogg to Ellen G. White, April 21, 1892, Ellen G. White Estate.
75 John Harvey Kellogg to Willie C. White, August 7, 1895, Ellen G. White Estate.
76 John Harvey Kellogg to J. D. Hare, M.D., June 15, 1892.
77 Ibid.
78 John Harvey Kellogg to Willie C. White, June 20, 1892, Ellen G. White Estate.
79 Ibid.
80 Ibid.
81 Ibid., August 7, 1895.

preaching and tract distribution."⁸² He indicated this was especially true in his home state of Michigan, which he described as being "a closed state to our workers … It is as difficult for our workers to get access to the people in Michigan as it has been for our missionaries to get into Tibet. Very few of the young people of Michigan come to the Sanitarium to enter our courses. There are only three or four in our medical school. Our students come mostly from the western states. Those of our workers who are out at work among the churches find that the churches have been filled with animosity toward our work by the false representations which have been poured into their ears, chiefly by ministers who have labored among them. For many years Eld. Evans was president of this conference, and he always took a strong stand against our work. Now Eld. Durland has taken his place, and his position is even more opposed."⁸³

> "… for I know they are all excellent people, good men, and mean to do the right thing, but they do not understand us nor our work."

His relationship with the Michigan Conference became so strained that he decided to stop paying substantial tithes and offerings from the sanitarium into the conference treasury. Instead, he used the tithe money to send out missionaries to work discreetly in the churches of that conference. He added that the president of the Illinois Conference had misrepresented his work in Chicago.⁸⁴

"The most singular thing is that those who ought to help us in this reform work are doing their best to hamper us," he wrote in 1896. "From the General Conference office goes out every now and then some slanderous statement against us. The latest is that we were manufacturing foods that gave people Bright's disease.… But I do not feel any animosity toward them, for I know they are all excellent people, good men, and mean to do the right thing, but they do not understand us nor our work."⁸⁵

"Our conferences will not recognize this work as a regular part of the work," he wrote as relations worsened. "They will not support it with their means, that is, the conference authorities will not—they must save all the money for the preachers, and will not contribute anything to the support of our evangelistic nurses and physicians who go out to work among them. They will not even pay the traveling expenses of a doctor who travels perhaps five hundred miles to get to the campmeeting, though he works every minute while on the ground, looking after the sick and giving advice that is worth to them many hundreds of dollars."⁸⁶

Exceptions to this statement were Wisconsin and Texas. Both conferences "agree to support some

---

82   John Harvey Kellogg to Ellen G. White, September 5, 1895, Ellen G. White Estate.
83   Ibid., April 14, 1898.
84   Ibid.
85   Ibid., December 16,, 1896.
86   Ibid., April 25, 1898.

of these workers, but the majority of the conferences will not take hold of the work."[87] By the fall of 1898 the negative attitude seemed to change and Illinois, Indiana, Ohio, Nebraska, and Kansas, among other states, had asked for workers. Even the Michigan Conference brethren decided to turn their Detroit mission into a medical mission.[88]

In the midst of all of this, he was caught in a struggle between two boards. The Foreign Mission Board sending out overseas missionaries and the Medical Missionary Board sending out the medical missionaries. The Foreign Mission Board paid all missionaries and thus claimed jurisdiction over them though they knew nothing of medical missionary work.[89] "There will be a determined effort to break down the Medical Missionary Board," he wrote early in 1899. "Eld. Moon and other members of the F. M. Board are determined that they shall rule over our doctors and nurses… The three active members of the Foreign Mission Board—Elders Moon, Jayne, and Edwards, are not at all in sympathy with this work and know nothing about it."[90]

Ellen White affirmed the trouble he had in working with ministers. In a letter to Kellogg dated April 17, 1899, she wrote, "The light given me of God, which I have written to Brother Moon and to Brother Irwin, and which they can show you, was that they should have helped you, that you should counsel together, that in the place of holding themselves aloof, they should have been your fellow helpers; that you were ordained by God to stand in a position of trust, that as you used your talents, God increased them, and that you needed help instead of censure."

In a letter to Elders Prescott, Irwin, Jones, Smith, and Waggoner, she wrote, "Our people have not all appreciated as they should the man through whom God has worked, and with whom He has cooperated upon the subject of health reform. They have not reasoned from cause to effect to understand how great was the blessing of the Sanitarium at Battle Creek under the management of Dr. Kellogg and his faithful associates. Through this work the truths of the third angel's message have entered where it would otherwise have been very difficult for them to find entrance."[91]

In spite of the opposition, it may have been good for him and the sanitarium. "The institution has prospered in spite of all these efforts against us, but it has been in spite of the influence of those who ought to be its friends rather than by their aid. I confess that this fact has had a tendency to alienate me from the church and to weaken my confidence sometimes, not because there are evil-minded and unwise persons in the church, but because these persons are allowed by the authorities of the church to go on in their evil work of mischief-making and slander against an institution which is represented to be one of the branches of the cause of God, without any attempt to check it."[92]

In 1897, he wrote, "It seems incomprehensible that men should get so exalted in their own

---

87 Ibid.
88 Ibid., September 18, 1898.
89 Ibid., April 14, 1897.
90 Ibid., January 5, 1899.
91 Ellen G. White, *Battle Creek Letters*, p. 14.
92 John Harvey Kellogg to Ellen G. White, December 6, 1886, Ellen G. White Estate.

estimation as to form conceptions that a preacher is so much superior to a doctor, or a doctor so much inferior to a preacher, that the doctor or a company of even Christian doctors, would not be capable of directing their own work, in which they have been trained for years, while the preacher, who has had no experience in the work whatever, becomes, by virtue of his ministerial license, competent to direct the physician or the nurse."[93]

But good came out of it. "I think I am not blind to the fact that all this persecution has been on the whole a good thing for the institution, and has contributed to our prosperity in certain ways, by making us more vigilant, and by stimulating those engaged in the work here to greater efforts in behalf of the institution."[94]

"You must not forget that our work here in the Sanitarium, in the preparation of medical missionaries, has been a voluntary one, organized and carried on without any official sanction or instruction from the General Conference Committee, as a committee."[95] Further down in his letter to Willie White, he wrote "The attitude of the people, and especially of our leading brethren, toward our work at the Sanitarium, ignoring it almost entirely for years at a time. This has had its influence upon our workers here, even upon our managers."[96]

In answering the objection of some young people losing their spirituality at the Sanitarium, he replied that some had also lost their way while working at the Review and Herald publishing plant.

Exceptions to the challenges he experienced with the church brethren were found in the support of O. A. Olsen, president of the General Conference, and Percy Magan, a young college professor who was helpful in teaching Bible to the sanitarium patients. He reported a great interest in health and temperance work among the 3,000 attendees at the 1892 Michigan summer camp meeting thanks to the influence of Elder Olsen.[97]

But Ellen White didn't accept apathy of the church leadership to medical missionary work as an excuse for Kellogg to detach himself from the church organization.

"Do not, I beg of you, instill into the minds of the students ideas that will cause them to lose confidence in God's appointed ministers," she wrote to him in 1898. "But this you are doing, whether you are aware of it or not. In His providence the Lord has placed you in a position where you may do a good work for Him in connection with the gospel ministry, bringing the truth before many who otherwise would not become acquainted with it. Temptations will come to you to think that in order to carry forward the medical missionary work you must stand aloof from the church organization or church discipline. To stand thus would place you on an unsound footing. The work done for those who come to you for instruction is not complete unless they are educated to work in connection with the church."[98]

---

93   Ibid., May 4, 1897.
94   Ibid., December 6, 1886.
95   John Harvey Kellogg to Willie C. White, June 20, 1892, Ellen G. White Estate.
96   Ibid.
97   John Harvey Kellogg to Ellen G. White, October 3, 1892, Ellen G. White Estate.
98   Ellen G. White, *Counsels on Health*, pp. 522, 523.

Ellen White wrote that "Dr. Kellogg's ideas and plans have not been of heavenly origin. For the past twenty years the church has been distracted in regard to the proper relation of the medical work to the gospel ministry, because Dr. Kellogg has been holding up the gospel minister as inferior to the medical missionary work."[99]

> "If the Lord does not wish us to care for so many people here, why does he send them to us?"

In addition to reprimanding Kellogg, Ellen White also spoke against the ministers. "It is a fact that our ministers are very slow to become health reformers, notwithstanding all the light which the Lord has given upon this subject. This has caused Dr. Kellogg to lose confidence in them. Their tardy work in health reform has crested in him a spirit of criticism, and he has borne down on them in an unsparing manner, which the Lord does not sanction. He has belittled the gospel ministry, and in his regard and ideas has placed the medical missionary work above the ministry."[100]

His passion for medical missionary work became so all consuming that he apparently tended to lose sight of church work as a whole. "You would make the medical missionary work the body and not the arm."[101]

Rebuilding Battle Creek

Investing so much energy in Battle Creek with large buildings drew many complaints from Ellen White. "In our conversation I spoke to you of the light given me that we are centering too many weighty responsibilities in Battle Creek, and I am of this same opinion now.... There is danger that it will become as Jerusalem of old, a concentrated, powerful center. The evils that ruined Jerusalem will come upon us if we do not heed these precautions. It is perilous to so largely center in Battle Creek; for while we are expending means in this one center, you are neglecting cities that will become more and more difficult to work as time goes on."[102]

Ellen White compared Kellogg to a famous Old Testament king. "The record of Nebuchadnezzar's life has been presented to me again and again to present to you, that you may be warned not to trust in yourself and your own wisdom, or to make flesh you arm."[103]

In spite of the warnings, the Battle Creek Sanitarium continued to thrive. In 1895 he wrote of 1,000 persons composing the entire family there, with 700 to 800 during the winter and spring and 1,100 to 1,200 during the summer, many of them influential professional people. They needed a chapel for lectures, especially during cooler weather when meeting on the lawn was difficult.

---

99   Ellen G. White, *Manuscript Releases*, vol. 21, p. 417.
100 Ellen G. White, *Battle Creek Letters*, p. 13.
101 Ibid., p. 20.
102 Ellen G. White, *Manuscript Releases*, vol. 7, p. 351.
103 Ibid., vol. 21, p. 53.

"If the Lord does not wish us to care for so many people here, why does he send them to us?" he asked. "We must have branch Sanitariums in other places, but we must first have doctors to take charge of them.... The establishment of small Sanitariums in different states will not diminish our work here—it will rather increase it. Every institution of this sort will be an advertisement of our work at Battle Creek."[104] He wanted to see new sanitariums started in New England and two points in the South as well as the St. Paul-Minneapolis area.[105]

The turn of the century brought a change of fortunes to Kellogg, and his attitude and relationship to Ellen White became more public. On February 18, 1902, the Battle Creek Sanitarium burned to the ground, destroying $350,000 worth of property, with $150,000 in insurance coverage.[106] Famed songwriter and singing evangelist Ira D. Sankey barely escaped.

A month after the fire, Kellogg wrote to Ellen White, "We have been waiting anxiously for some providential indication as to our duty about rebuilding here at Battle Creek. The Lord seems to be opening the way for us by awakening the people to an appreciation of the Sanitarium and its principles and it now looks as though we shall begin the work of rebuilding within a short time."[107]

In June he went to Europe to encourage the medical missionaries there. In a letter to Ellen White, Kellogg said that while he had been too busy to write, he had forwarded materials to her to keep her informed about developments at Battle Creek. The main focus of the letter certainly had nothing to do with Battle Creek. Instead, he reported news of the Adventist medical missionary work in Europe. The Queen of England with her father, the king of Denmark, her sister, the ex-empress of Russia, and Prince Aldemar, brother of the ex-empress of Russia, visited the Skodsborg Sanitarium in Copenhagen.

"The Queen of England inquired very earnestly of our work and asked if we had an institution in England, and was glad to know we were going to have one," he wrote. "They spent quite a part of one afternoon in the institution, and the Queen's last remark, as she was leaving, was 'This is an exceedingly interesting work, isn't it?'"[108]

His next comment perhaps showed his drive for credibility with Ellen White and the church. "The Lord is doing wonderful things in opening the way for the work."[109]

By August 1902 the building project of the new sanitarium in Battle Creek was well underway. Thinking Ellen White may have been misinformed about the size of the new institution, Kellogg wrote that the building was going to be 525 feet long, which was 175 feet shorter than the old one, with 288 guest rooms, fewer than in the old building, and accommodating 350 people. He hoped for a campus with many small buildings.

By his words Kellogg seemed to defend the size of the first sanitarium. "The work in Battle Creek

---

104 John Harvey Kellogg to Ellen G. White, September 5, 1895, Ellen G. White Estate.
105 Ibid.
106 Ibid., November 2, 1902.
107 Ibid., March 20, 1902.
108 Ibid., June 27, 1902.
109 Ibid.

grew to large proportions because of the lack of trained physicians to deal with the sick elsewhere," he added, citing that he had trouble finding young men and women wanting to become physicians to work in other cities.[110]

Even before the completion of the new sanitarium building, patients began pouring in. "We have among our patients, putting up with great inconveniences, persons who are worth millions," he wrote. "They have been sent here by governors and prominent physicians, and are willing to put up with any sort of emergency accommodations for the time being in the hope of something better later."[111]

He seemed to have a good reason for staying put in Battle Creek. "If we had undertaken to have moved away, we should have had to begin at the bottom, as the insurance money and the property we had left was only sufficient to pay our debts," he wrote. "We were only able to start the new building here in Battle Creek by the donations of the citizens, the confidence and goodwill of the bankers who advanced us the necessary means, and the use of the buildings and the property which the fire did not destroy and which would have been of no use to us if we had moved away."[112]

The new facility opened at the end of May 1903 with "no burden to the denomination," as Kellogg stated.[113] In a letter to Ellen White in which he outlined the dedication of the new facility, he wrote, "We all recognize that the instruction you have given us is light from Heaven, and that it is exactly what we need."[114] He also stated that "our fire has created a wonderful wave of sympathy for our work,"[115] after sharing with her that the governor and prominent state officials planned to attend. The president of the United States was among the invitees.

In all of this Kellogg did not directly consult Ellen White about whether or not to rebuild the sanitarium in Battle Creek. In an effort to repair relations with her he wrote the following in October 1903, after the sanitarium opened, regarding why he had not written to her regarding the decision to rebuild. "I talked the matter over with Dr. Paulson and others, and we decided that the proper thing for us to do was to place the matter before the Lord and leave it for him to communicate to you such light as was best for us, and trust him to send it to us in such time and way as was in accordance with his will." Then in a stunning admission, he added, "Evidently we made a mistake."[116]

In the same letter, he confirmed what she said about accumulating too many helpers in one place, but Kellogg requested that Ellen White spend some time at Battle Creek to see the situation firsthand.[117]

In November 1903 he again tried to justify rebuilding the Battle Creek Sanitarium without consulting Ellen White. "If I had got a letter from you before we began building the Battle Creek Sanitarium

---

110 Ibid., August 25, 1902.
111 Ibid., between January 5 and February 15, 1903.
112 Ibid.
113 Ibid., February 15, 1903.
114 Ibid., May 19, 1903.
115 Ibid.
116 Ibid., October 18, 1903.
117 Ibid.

to the effect that we should not erect a large building here in Battle Creek I am sure we never should have done it," he wrote. "When I called the brethren in council to advise us, if any of them had said we should not move without writing to Sister White, we should certainly have done so. It is evident that we made a great mistake in not writing, and have had no end of trouble and perplexities because we didn't."[118]

He added that he wanted harmony, unity, and peace so things could progress with the medical missionaries and ministers working hand in hand. At the end of this same letter, Kellogg's choice of words seemed to indicate that he viewed Ellen White as more of an influential individual than as a prophetess. "I know the Lord has made you the leader of this people and this work, and I feel grateful for the light I have received through you."[119]

To help raise money for the new sanitarium and pay for what was not covered by the insurance money, Kellogg had written *The Living Temple*. While the leading brethren had committed themselves not to ask church members to pay for a new sanitarium, they had agreed to promote *The Living Temple* as a fundraising venture.[120]

But the book brought its own set of problems. "As regards *The Living Temple*, I think I see where the trouble is," he wrote to her late in 1903. "I was very willing and anxious to have it right, but I did not understand where the trouble was… The one point in the book that I was anxious to maintain was the fact that you bring out so beautifully in your new book on Education, that man's life comes from God, and that all his bodily functions are under control of this life."[121]

He added that he had put the book in the hands of Professor Prescott and Elder Jones to revise and would accept all their criticisms as well as that of Elder Haskell. He told Willie White that he had organized a corps of people to sell *The Living Temple* but had the project on hold until a satisfactory resolution could be agreed upon. In the meantime, he would put his people to work selling Ellen White's new book *Education*.

He admitted the shortcomings of *The Living Temple*. "It is evident that I blundered greatly in writing The Living Temple in saying anything at all about the personality of God. I ought simply to have presented the idea of God in nature, and have permitted the Lord to deal with the rest of the question in each individual man."[122]

During *The Living Temple* controversy, business at the sanitarium continued to boom, and Kellogg wanted Ellen White to see it firsthand. "We have several hundred patients here who will be glad to see you." He added that several delegates to The National Academy of Sciences meeting in Chicago were planning to visit the sanitarium on their way home, thanks to the influence of one of their prominent

---

118   Ibid., November 12, 1903.
119   Ibid.
120   Ibid., November 2, 1902.
121   Ibid., October 24, 1903.
122   Ibid., November 15, 1903.

members who was interested in diet reform.[123]

It was during this time that Kellogg admitted his own sense of spiritual drift and the strained medical-ministerial relations that were mounting. He recalled some of the great lessons he had learned at the righteousness by faith revival in Minneapolis years before, saying, "In this medical missionary work I know that I have gradually drifted away from this simple faith which trusts absolutely in the merits of Christ, and in His power to use and move the human agent just as an instrument is moved in a man's hand; and as a consequence I know but little in my own personal experience of today what Christ meant when He said: 'Come unto Me, all ye that are weary and heavy laden and I will give you rest.'"[124]

At the end of 1903, in a letter to Willie White, he agreed to publish the physiological part of *The Living Temple* under another title as advised by Ellen White and cut out everything regarded as theological in nature. He chose *The Miracle of Life* as the title of the new book. He noted that two or three thousand copies of *The Living Temple* had been sold but had been returned after the condemnation of the book. He suggested he could cut out the objectionable pages and resell them to patients, where there was a demand. Some of them wanted to use the book as Christmas presents.[125]

Almost two years after the reopening of the sanitarium, Kellogg still felt the need to justify the decision to stay in Battle Creek. "I am not at all in favor of a large city sanitarium," he wrote to Ellen White in 1905. "I have wished a hundred times that the Battle Creek Sanitarium was in a quiet country place, away from city smoke and sounds, although Battle Creek is a very small village; but I did not locate the institution there in the first place. I took it as I found it, and I have done the best I could to make a success, and that the Lord has blessed and prospered the institution there, nobody can deny."[126]

Leaving the Church

The next few years were unhappy for Kellogg. In a letter to G. I. Butler, he indicated that he felt people were misrepresenting him to Ellen White "in the grossest kind of way."[127]

He parted company with the church in 1907, not for pantheism but for "non support of the church, non belief in the testimonies and for nonattendance."[128]

A thriving Battle Creek Sanitarium kept Kellogg afloat despite the challenges he had with Ellen White and the church. While the believers at Loma Linda were making heroic sacrifices to start a medical school there, with the blessing of Ellen White, Kellogg remained in Battle Creek and took care of famous people such as William Jennings Bryan, Harry Byrd, and William Gibbs McAdoo, son-in-law and adviser to President Woodrow Wilson.

---

123 Ibid.
124 Ibid., November 25, 1903.
125 John Harvey Kellogg to Willie C. White, December 6, 1903, Ellen G. White Estate.
126 John Harvey Kellogg to Ellen G. White, March 21, 1905, Ellen G. White Estate.
127 John Harvey Kellogg to G. I. Butler, November 5, 1905, Ellen G. White Estate.
128 Jim McKinley, "John Harvey Kellogg: A Controversy 1897-1907" (term paper, Andrews University, Seventh-day Adventist Theological Seminary, Berrien Springs, MI, December 1978), p. 23.

His younger brother, W .K. Kellogg, went into the cereal business and built the world-famous Kellogg Foods. Charles W. Post, a former san patient, became an overnight millionaire exploiting the commercial possibilities of the food formulas he learned about while a patient at the Battle Creek Sanitarium.

While Ellen White was declining in health at Elmshaven, California, in deep perplexity over the future of Loma Linda, which she said would eclipse Battle Creek as the center of Adventist medical work, John Harvey Kellogg prospered by going interdenominational.

Kellogg entertained many notable individuals. People like Professor Irving Fisher of Yale University; Edmund Ball of Muncie, Indiana, manufacturer of Ball Jars; Joel E. Cheek of Nashville, brewer of Maxwell House Coffee; Harry M. Daugherty, attorney general in the Harding administration; fruit juice mogul E. T. Welch; entertainer Eddie Cantor; naturalist Luther Burbank; and educator Booker T. Washington came to the sanitarium. Other distinguished guests included Harvey Firestone, Homer Rodeheaver, S. S. McClure, George Bernard Shaw, and Henry Ford. Amelia Earhart and George Palmer Putnam took him for a 10-minute airplane ride over Battle Creek.

Funk & Wagnalls heiress Lida Scott, by now a major financial supporter of Percy Magan in developing the College of Medical Evangelists, wrote to him that "Mr. Scott [her husband] had a conversation with Dr. Kellogg in New York, having had him out to lunch, in which Dr. Kellogg said the standard of Loma Linda would never be raised, and that the Medical Association would never stand for a denominational medical college; so when Mr. Scott brought the information home I was glad I could say quietly, 'It has already been raised.' [to a B rating] Mr. Scott was astonished, and I think since then he has realized that Dr. Kellogg's word is not necessarily final. From a remark he made the other night I can see that he thinks Dr. Kellogg is prejudiced against our people."[129]

In another letter to Magan, Scott said Kellogg had told her husband that Ellen White was a plagiarist.[130]

When Loma Linda finally received its A rating from the American Medical Association in 1922, Kellogg showed his medical missionary side in a letter to Magan, dean of the Los Angeles campus.

"Certainly you are to be congratulated that you have obtained the A grade at last for your school. Providence has seemed to favor your schemes, especially in the working out of the Southern California Medical School and by giving you an opportunity to demand recognition which you otherwise might not have gotten. Now if you will only raise your standard so as to make sure that the men and women who go out from your school are real missionaries and not merely commercial doctors, you may accomplish something really worthwhile, but if you run a medical school which is not radically different from other medical schools in the country, it will not be worthwhile. I think you ought to make your students feel that it is a criminal thing for them to use the advantages which have been secured through the self-sacrificing of hundreds of honest men and women merely to prepare themselves for a

---

129 Lida F. Scott to Percy T. Magan, January 25, 1918, Center for Adventist Research, Berrien Springs, Michigan.
130 Ibid., July 6, 1917.

money-getting vocation. Such a course looks to me like down right thievery. Every one of your students ought to go out as an apostle of health reform and medical reform. It is not worthwhile to bother with any others."

His final comment seemed to echo the guidelines of Ellen White. "You better have a small school and have the kind of men who will be leaders when they will go out than to have a large school with low standards and an indifferent sort of graduates."[131]

While he encouraged Loma Linda to remain small, he enlarged the Battle Creek Sanitarium during the booming 1920s by adding a four-story dining room wing and a fifteen-story tower. On the surface, it vindicated his nonsectarian, interdenominational success formula. While Loma Linda was small, he was world famous. By 1935 more than 300,000 patients had come to Battle Creek.

If the Great Depression had not come along in 1929, Kellogg might have showed how a creative, energetic doctor could pay off a multimillion-dollar debt by going interdenominational. Perhaps he could have said the Lord had brought all these famous people to his san and would not let anything bad happen to it. And perhaps he would not have had to sell it to the Federal Government for use as a veteran's hospital during World War II.

Kellogg started out strong, but he had trouble putting religious faith over pragmatism. He followed the health principles of Ellen White and went to medical school at her behest. But he balked at doing things not readily apparent to the ordinary person, like downsizing the Battle Creek Sanitarium or encouraging his people to start smaller sanitariums in many places. He could see that doing what Ellen White said would hurt his popularity. What was good for the church was not always best for the Battle Creek business community. The Battle Creek Sanitarium was a priceless economic resource for them. A big place impresses people more than many small places.

His problem involved more than following her administrative counsel. He also struggled with accepting her instructions as visions from God. At times his comments seemed to indicate that she might be speaking through the influence of those around her like her son Willie or powerful people like A. G. Daniells. Kellogg seemed to feel his ideas were as good as Ellen White's. As a result, he tended to view science and medicine with higher validity than the Bible or the gift of prophecy. He also seemed to view himself as superior to the denominational ministers. As a result, Daniells was able to make a caricature out of Kellogg and eliminate him from denominational life. Had Kellogg adhered to Ellen White, he might have brought out some of Daniells' weaknesses. Instead, the opposite happened.

Kellogg's life story shows that talent, education, energy, dedication, prominence, and enterprise are wonderful blessings but are no substitute for following divine directions.

---

131 John Harvey Kellogg to Percy T. Magan, December 5, 1922, Center for Adventist Research, Berrien Springs, Michigan.

A Profile of Arthur G. Daniells:

A Ministry Without Physicians

Arthur Grosvenor Daniells was born in West Union, Iowa, on September 28, 1858, the eldest son of Thomas Grosvenor and Mary Jane McQuillain-Daniells. His physician father died during the Civil War.

He was baptized at the age of thirteen during a camp meeting at Marion, Iowa, and he started active work in the Seventh-day Adventist Church at the age of sixteen by selling a "Health Almanac" published by Elder James White. He entered Battle Creek College in 1875 but only studied there one year because of poor health.

Like William Miller, James White, Abe Lincoln, and Mark Twain, he did not enjoy the advantage of a college education, but that did not stop him from working for the Lord and eventually becoming General Conference president of the Seventh-day Adventist Church.

He married Mary Ellen Hoyt soon after dropping out of college and started denominational work in Texas in 1878 under Robert M. Kilgore and then served as a secretary to James and Ellen White.

His ministerial career started in his home state of Iowa, with the Review and Herald announcing in the June 24, 1880, edition that the conference had granted him a ministerial license at its seventeenth annual camp meeting in Des Moines.

The next year he and Ira. J. Hankins wrote about conducting a series of meetings in Sumner, Iowa. Later on, writing from West Union, Iowa, he shared with *Review* readers that two of his original converts had given up their new faith, but eight had remained. They organized a Sabbath School of twenty members.[1]

---

1   *The Review and Herald,* April 11, 1882, p. 236.

In 1882 he was ordained to the gospel ministry at the annual Iowa camp meeting.[2]

Various leadership appointments followed, including director of District No. 1 in the Iowa Conference and member of the executive committee of the Iowa Sabbath School Convention.

He also conducted meetings in many Iowa towns. His District No. 1 consisted of churches in West Union, Sumner, Hazelton, Elgin, Waukon, and Lansing.

A few years later, a ten-year-old girl named Edith Howard wrote to *The Youth's Instructor* that Daniells and Hankins had baptized her parents five years before in Marshalltown, Iowa.[3]

In the October 13, 1885, edition of the *Review*, he wrote a brief note about the importance of Adventist literature, in this instance promoting the sale of *Thoughts on Daniel and the Revelation* by Uriah Smith. He also represented Iowa at the 1885 General Conference session, the first of many he would be part of. Here his name appeared as a member of the Committee on City Missions, which made recommendations for working metropolitan areas.[4] In 1886, he accepted other leadership positions, which included serving as president of the Iowa Health and Temperance Association and secretary-treasurer of the Iowa Conference.

Serving Overseas

Then, in October 1886, the General Conference sent Mr. and Mrs. Daniells to New Zealand. While serving overseas, he showed exceptional leadership and organizational abilities in following up the work of S. N. Haskell the year before.

"We sailed from San Francisco Oct. 24, in the steamboat *Alameda*," he announced to *Review* readers. "A company of brethren and sisters from Oakland were at the wharf to see us off. Their presence and good words of cheer were a help to us as we started on this our first ocean voyage."[5]

They went first to Honolulu, then crossed 8,800 miles of ocean to Auckland, New Zealand, arriving on November 14. He stayed at the home of Brother Edward Hare and described Auckland as having 65,000 mostly English-speaking people and five Sabbathkeepers. Another company of believers, the first Seventh-day Adventist Church in New Zealand, which had been organized by S. N. Haskell in 1885, met 150 miles away in a city named Kaeo.

"The prospects are that we shall have opposition from the clergy," he predicted. "But notwithstanding this, and our inability to do anything for the Lord without his help, we are of good courage. We believe the God of Israel will work for us here."[6]

During his first series of meetings there, Daniells baptized fifteen people, the same number as Haskell after his initial visit, and organized a church by ordaining an elder and deacon as well as electing

---

2 *The Review and Herald,* June 13, 1882, p. 377.
3 *The Youth's Instructor,* July 2, 1890, p. 108.
4 *The Review and Herald,* December 1, 1885.
5 *The Review and Herald,* January 4, 1887, p. 13.
6 Ibid.

a committee of three to oversee work in the colony.[7]

Daniells' evangelistic meetings in Auckland also made an impact, with a growing attendance and twenty to thirty people starting to keep the Sabbath. He reported that the mainline ministers feared Adventism was there to stay.[8]

"We enjoyed laboring with Eld. Daniells and wife very much," wrote Will D. Curtis after visiting them in Auckland. "The Lord is crowning their efforts with success. A good class of people have accepted the truth as the result of their labors."[9]

The next year's report showed young Daniells, now twenty-nine years old, growing in leadership as well as evangelistic ability. "As the result of the tent-meetings in Auckland, New Zealand, by Bro. Daniells, thirty persons have signed the covenant, and four or five others have begun the observance of the Sabbath. The house of worship erected by the church there, 'as neat and comfortable as any in the city,' has been completed at a cost of about $2,000, and is nearly free from debt. At the quarterly meeting out of a membership of eighty-four, seventy-six responded."[10]

The next year, on May 27, 1889, a general meeting of Seventh-day Adventists in the colony elected Daniells as the first president of the New Zealand Conference. He reported 200 persons observing the Sabbath there, 100 of whom were church members, and a treasury surplus of $240.[11] This same meeting, with Daniells as chair, also organized a tract and missionary society to promote literature sale and distribution.[12]

"We have the fullest liberty to sell our publications anywhere in the colony," Daniells informed *Review* readers. Other advantages of the isolated New Zealand field were favorable newspaper coverage of the church and easy availability of the best public auditoriums because of a large public curiosity about Adventism. He also was glad to report that four of their young men planned to attend Healdsburg and Battle Creek colleges in the United States to better prepare themselves for the Lord's work in the antipodes.[13]

At the end of 1890, Daniells transferred to Australia. "We have sustained quite a loss in the removal of Elder Daniells to Australia," commented James Harris, head book agent, in the *Review*. "Since his advent to the colony, God has abundantly blessed his labors. Through his instrumentality the cause has been established, and quite a company of workers organized to carry on the work so successfully started. Our loss is Australia's gain, and we pray that God will bless him and his wife in their new field."[14]

---

7   *The Review and Herald,* February 8, 1887, p. 91.
8   Ibid., May 3, 1887, p. 284.
9   Ibid., August 23, 1887, p. 539.
10 Ibid., July 17, 1888, p. 456.
11 Ibid., August 27, 1889, p. 541.
12 Ibid., September 3, 1889, pp. 555, 556.
13 *Advent Review and Sabbath Herald*, September 24, 1889, p. 603.
14 Ibid., May 26, 1891, p. 331.

He started working in Ballarat, Melbourne, and Sydney one year before Ellen White and her entourage moved to Australia. Daniells thus became well acquainted with the Whites, but he never seemed to get too close to Ellen White, much as he believed in her testimonies as the following letter indicates.

"I have read the testimony which you sent me many times, and have endeavored to do so with a prayerful heart," he wrote to her in 1895. "Some portions I do not as yet understand. Other parts are plain. I do not cast any of it aside, but pray the Lord to help me to be admonished by it all. Some of the points I would like to write about, but I do not know as it would be right to do so. I am sorry that I have not counseled with you more about the perplexities of my work, but at first I thought it would burden you too much, and later I have felt that you would not care to be troubled with me. But I feel that my course has increased your burdens, and now if you are willing I feel that I should like to write you freely with reference to the plans we are trying to carry."[15]

The move to Australia placed him in a position to exert wider influence. "It seems natural that Australia should become the base of operations for much of the southern world, if not all of our work in Asia. All the missionary societies operating in Polynesia have their headquarters in Sydney, and it would seem that our own work in these islands could be prosecuted from this point more readily than from San Francisco."[16]

The 550-member Australian Conference elected Daniells to be its president at its 1892 constituency meeting. Here again, he gave lots of attention to the publishing work.

"Elder Daniells was chosen to the presidency of the Conference and tract society, and steps were taken to bring the latter into a more active condition than heretofore. Colportage is to be prosecuted as a means of following up the interest which has been created by the sale of books."[17]

Literature sale and distribution formed the heart of Daniells' program in Australasia, as he termed the island region consisting of Australia, New Zealand, Tasmania, Norfolk, New Guinea, New Britain, and the Solomon group. He described it as a productive country with a complex population "from the cultivated man of Oxford and Cambridge, to the ignorant, naked savages of New Guinea." In the same article, he wrote, "Drinking, gambling, and racing are huge evils in Australasia.... And now a strong current of public sentiment is setting in for a closer union of religion and politics."[18]

And how was the church to reach these diverse pleasure lovers in the Southern Hemisphere? "To do for others what we should, will require self-denial and earnest labor," he proclaimed. "We must put forth unceasing labor to show them the light, and lead them to walk in it. We shall find it necessary to give our means and ourselves to the work. The message must be proclaimed publicly in our cities and towns.... Printed matter must be placed in the hands of all, that they may learn what God has to say to

---

15   A. G. Daniells to Ellen G. White, March 3, 1895, Ellen G. White Estate.
16   *Advent Review and Sabbath Herald,* November 17, 1891, p. 715.
17   Ibid., March 8, 1892, p. 152.
18   Ibid., December 12, 1893, pp. 777, 778.

them. All this will require preachers, colporteurs, Bible workers ... papers, books, tracts and funds."[19]

In September 1894, Willie White sent some impressive reports to the *Review*, including that Daniells has held three successful meetings in the Paramatta town hall.[20] Daniells just seemed to do everything right.

O. A. Olsen, president of the General Conference from 1888 to 1897, visited the 1894 camp meeting, the first of its kind ever held in Australia, and found nearly 500 people encamped in suburban Melbourne. "To the citizens of Melbourne this large encampment, with fine new tents and so large a gathering of people from all over these colonies, comes as the greatest surprise possible," Olsen wrote. "They do not know how to take it or how to account for it.... Elder Daniells, the president of the Conference, has borne up remarkably under the continuous strain and the heavy burdens connected with this meeting. The Lord has blessed him in a very special manner."[21]

That year marked a milestone in the development of the Adventist church organization. The church was becoming more of an international body, and it needed a responsive structure to address growing needs in such faraway places as Australia and South Africa. Going to Battle Creek to make key decisions wasted time. The Australasian Conference meeting at Middle Brighton, Victoria, early in 1894, took the first step at diversifying authority by organizing a union conference. That session also took up the matter of building a training school for the Australasian field.

In her weekly article for the *Review*, Ellen White wrote in the January 7, 1896, edition of how Daniells was following one of her guidelines in his work there in Australia. She said that "our brethren," presumably led by Daniells, wanted to conduct their third camp meeting to help out a struggling church in Ballarat, "a city of thirty thousand people, about ninety miles north from Melbourne....

"But the Lord has been giving me light about the work to be done in our large cities," she continued. "The people in the cities are to be warned, and the message should go to them now... The interest which began to be awakened by the camp meeting held two years ago in Brighton, should be carried forward by a camp-meeting in some part of Melbourne each year. When the brethren took these things into consideration, they decided that the meeting should be held in Melbourne, and in their search for a ground were led to locate in Armadale ... a locality convenient to densely populated suburbs where the message had never been given."[22]

She was very pleased with the size and quality of the crowd coming, as well as the twenty people baptized. "Camp-meetings are a success in arresting the attention of the people," she concluded.[23]

This camp meeting also saw the division of the 1,125-member Australian Conference, which covered a huge territory, into two territories, with Willie White as president in New South Wales and Daniells as president of the Central Australian Conference, consisting of South Australia, Victoria, and

---

19   Ibid.
20   Ibid., September 11, 1894, p. 532.
21   Ibid., March 6, 1894, p. 152.
22   Ibid., *Advent Review and Sabbath Herald*, January 7, 1896, pp. 3, 4.
23   Ibid.

Tasmania. They set apart Queensland and West Australia as General Conference missions. Tithe coming in was sufficient to meet their financial needs.[24]

Success of the Australian camp meetings seemed to grow, with the end of 1896 seeing ones in Adelaide with 300 to 500 people attending and another one in Melbourne and then in Sydney.

Daniells didn't have any trouble following Ellen White's camp meeting guidelines. "I look with the deepest interest and with much fear and trembling to the five camp meetings we propose to hold during the coming year," he wrote to her. "I greatly desire that the Lord will teach us the importance of these meetings and how to manage them and follow up the interest as we should. We know that there is a great deal of hard work and heavy expenses connected with a camp meeting, but if rightly managed I feel sure that it is a wise investment. I intend to read with care what you have written about camp meetings and how to properly manage them. I would be very grateful to receive any suggestions from you. You have attended all the camp meetings held in this country, and have observed the different features of management. If you have been impressed with reference to any special points where our committees can make improvement I hope that you will feel free to let us know."[25]

In another letter to Ellen White, Daniells wrote that the Union Conference Committee wanted to make a supreme effort to hold camp meetings in the large cities of the different colonies during the summer of 1896 and 1897. To pay for it, each conference could assign its workers to canvass six months a year.

He showed his high-powered organization skills in telling a Brother Starr how to run one of the camp meetings. "And now Dear Brother let me suggest a pointer," he wrote. "When you start your next camp meeting, organize your camp at the beginning and make thorough plans for running the camp meeting into a rousing tent mission. No time should be lost in the change from the camp to the tent mission. We lose much in not organizing our work so that everything will be under the care of someone, and every one have some particular line to look after. Note how the Children of Israel were organized during their journeys in the wilderness. You can begin with the first and simplest duty of the day on the camp ground—the ringing of the bell. Appoint the ringer, give him the exact time for ringing and cause him to realize the importance of promptness in his work. Without this the movements of the campers must bring confusion—a state which God is not Author of. Then there are your chorister and choir, leaders of meetings, tent ushers, tent masters, sanitary committee, camp treasurer, pastoral committee, reporter and advertising agent etc. As I attend these meetings and see the painful confusion and loss that results from a failure to organize the camp forces I feel that we must make a decided change … But don't let organization take the place of good sense and the presence and power of the Spirit of God. It will never be able to supply their place. And I believe the Holy Spirit will never work much in the midst of the distraction and confusion that always exists where there is no organization."[26]

In approaching the end of his tenure in Australia, he perhaps showed he was almost ready to take

---

24   Ibid., February 4, 1896, p. 30.
25   A. G. Daniells to Ellen G. White, March 8, 1896, Ellen G. White Estate.
26   A. G. Daniells to Brother Starr, January 10, 1900, Ellen G. White Estate.

the leadership of the world church in a letter to Brethren White and Palmer on guidelines for setting up a health food company.

"It seems to me that three principal parties should operate the entire business. I would name these parties as the Board of Management, the Business Manager, and the Field Agent. I think the Board should define a policy of management, engage employees, set wages and authorize expenditures. I think they should have a manager to purchase materials, superintend factory work, and direct the accountant. In purchasing materials he should give much study to the quality and the prices. Half the success of the business depends upon successful purchasing. He should have time to do this well. In superintending the factory he should see that every employee makes good use of every hour of time for which he is paid, and he should see that the quality of the goods manufactured is first class. He should also see that a sufficient stock is always ready to supply the orders that come in. In directing the accountant he should see that the shipping is promptly and accurately done, that bills are paid, and accounts collected. If all these details are successfully carried out the manager will be kept busy, and good work so far as the factory is concerned, will be done. And now comes in the work of the Field Agent who should be a rustler in soliciting orders, securing and directing agents, arranging for lectures and demonstrations, co-operating with the various agencies throughout the field, and working up literature, counter and window cards etc. It seems to me that only one general field agent working on a salary, should be employed for at least some time to come."[27]

In 1897 the General Conference divided its worldwide work into three grand divisions: the General Conference of North America, the European Union Conference, and the Australian Conference, each with its own president and executive committee. The North American Conference president would also serve as General Conference president at large. Daniells became president of the Australasian Conference; Willie White served as vice president.[28]

By 1899 Daniells could report a growing medical and educational work. "Our school enterprise and our medical work are both moving along encouragingly," he wrote. "I believe the Lord is leading out in these lines, to exercise a great influence not only in Australasia, but in other parts of the British Empire.... You would be very much surprised, and I think pleased, if you could visit the Avondale estate now. We have four buildings, which are a credit to us. They are plain and inexpensive, but neat. Our orchard is in a good condition."[29]

General Conference President George A. Irwin, while touring Australasia, noted that the publishing work had been the first there to develop, followed by education. Now with a college at Avondale in the making, the brethren there were turning their attention to building a sanitarium at the urging of Ellen White. He appealed to sister sanitariums in the world field to help with this need.[30]

Daniells continued following Ellen White's counsel to hold camp meetings. In a letter dated

---

27 A. G. Daniells to Willie C. White and Edwin R. Palmer, February 11, 1900, Ellen G. White Estate.
28 *Advent Review and Sabbath Herald*, March 16, 1897, p.170.
29 Ibid., July 11, 1899, p. 447.
30 Ibid., November 28, 1899, p. 775.

January 24, 1899, Daniells wrote to Ellen White and shared with her the great success of a Melbourne camp meeting. "The tent was packed as full as it could be, and hundreds remained outside. They would stand by the large tent, and listen until a shower would come, and then they would all scatter for the small tents, the dining tent, and the children's tent. In the evening we had a splendid congregation. I spoke on the coming crisis. The Spirit of the Lord rested upon us, and made the places very solemn.

"I have read portions to them of your new book, *The Desire of Ages*. These have made a deep impression on the minds of the brethren and sisters… I understand that between fifty and one hundred are coming from Melbourne tomorrow. It looks to me as though the camp meeting will have to be extended for one week."

Other camp meetings were also successful. Ellen White reported in the May 22, 1900, *Review* of one held at Geelong, Victoria, about fifty miles southwest of Melbourne, attracting as many as 1,500 people to some meetings. "The meeting this last Sunday evening surpassed anything we have before witnessed," she wrote. "In some respects it resembled the meetings held in 1843 and 1844."[31]

Daniells also followed Ellen White's counsel in the area of tithing. "I have been endeavouring for some time to get to work on the matter you have kindly placed in our hands on the 'Tithing System,' but I have been so overwhelmed with other matters, that it has seemed impossible to do this," he wrote. "I am in the fullest sympathy with what you have written with reference to getting out something on this subject to place in the hands of the people … I feel that we should place the subject of 'Systematic Benevolence' in its various forms before our people by articles in the Echo, Gleaner, small tracts, and circular letters. The cause greatly needs the funds, and the brethren and sisters greatly need the blessing that accompanies faithfulness in returning to the Lord His own."[32] Perhaps Daniells' best-known vindication of Ellen White counsel was when the Australian conference committee went ahead and purchased property for the Avondale school despite an unfavorable governmental report on the soil quality.

Leading the World Church

After the turn of the century, Daniells and Ellen White left Australia about the same time, she to make her home in California and he, on furlough for the first time, to help prepare for the 1901 General Conference session.

As he returned to the States, Daniells sensed an important and fruitful chapter of his career closing. Adventism in Australia had started from scratch in 1885, and after fifteen years, there were now ten ordained ministers, eighteen licensed preachers, twenty Bible workers, and seventy-five canvassers working in the country.

In a speech given upon leaving Australia in 1900, Daniells reflected on his time there. "Well, I realize that I am cutting loose from my work and friends in Australia," he contemplated. "I hardly realized that it would seem so much like leaving home. My feelings would lead me to leave the boat here, and

---

31   Ibid., May 22, 1900, p. 322.
32   A. G. Daniells to Ellen G. White, January 27, 1897, Ellen G. White Estate.

after making West Australia a good visit go back to where I started from. At the same time I feel the fullest assurance that I am in the path of duty. There are so many evidences of the Lord's leading that I am sure that this step is right, and that we shall see the reasons for it more clearly later on."

He then commented on what had made this extraordinary progress possible. "The disposition of the people to read has created an extensive opening for placing the message before them through the medium of literature. The blessing of the Lord is surely attending the canvassers who are traversing the length and breadth of these colonies with our books.

"Another great avenue opened before us for doing effective work in extending the message for this time, is the medical branch. Australasia, like all other countries, seems like a vast hospital. Wherever we turn we meet the sick and suffering seeking relief. Within our hands have been placed the most rational and efficient means in the world for the restoration of health. Whoever is prepared to administer these remedies is placed on great vantage ground for imparting a knowledge of the Third Angels Message."

The type of workers he listed as being needed included ministers, trained teachers, Bible workers of mature years and deep Christian experience, and God-fearing, efficient canvassers. All depended on faithful tithe and liberal gifts to support the workers and sustain and equip every branch of the work. But he did not mention physicians or medical personnel in this listing.

On his way to the United States, he travelled to Capetown with the wealthy John Wessels, whose family had earned a fortune from the South African diamond mines and who had at one time served as manager of the Adventist sanitarium in Australia. He spent three weeks with the Wessels and saw the Boer War firsthand, with the Wessels family having relatives on the losing Boer (Dutch) side. He also observed a serious financial crisis the Claremont Sanitarium in South Africa was going through.

The African sojourn clearly broadened his knowledge of the world field and its needs. On July 3, 1900, he wrote a detailed description of the Adventist work in Africa to Willie White, especially describing Basutoland and the Orange River Colony in tremendous depth.

He next traveled to London and turned his attention to learning about the Adventist work throughout Europe in preparation for the upcoming meetings of the General Conference Committee in October. His boat docked in New York City about the same time Ellen White arrived in San Francisco. Perhaps anticipating a prominent role in what lay ahead, Daniells asked her to attend the upcoming committee meetings that would help steer the 1901 General Conference session.

"There are many questions pertaining to the European and African fields that need immediate consideration, and I know we shall greatly need your presence … You (and Willie) have both been in Switzerland, Germany, Scandinavia and England. You personally know how the work ought to have been carried forward in those countries, and you could give us all sound counsel regarding plans that ought to be laid to push the work along with greater speed.

"In all my travels since leaving you I have seen everywhere the tendency to narrow down to the limits of our human capacity, instead of broadening out according to the greatness of the Lord's power to carry on His works. Unless there is a decided change in our plans to give this message to the world I do not see how any of us who are now living can expect to see it close up in our day. But little has been done in many of the European countries we have been working in for years, and even now we are working in the narrowest possible circle. The masses have not heard a word about the message. But in France, Italy, Spain, Portugal there has nothing been done worth referring to. Then there is China, also India with millions upon millions of people who are in utter darkness. As I look upon these whole nations for whom we have not yet begun to work scarcely, and then see how many workers we have employed in little conferences in the states and the money we are paying them to try to keep up the courage of faltering churches, my heart burns within me."[33]

Daniells proved to be at the center of action as the 1901 General Conference session got underway. General Conference President George A. Irwin announced that the canvassing work would have a prominent part in the discussions. Daniells' was to prepare a presentation titled "The Relation of Religious and Health Works. Is It Competition or Co-operation?"[34]

He had a lot to say about the reorganizational need. His experience in organizing local conferences and a larger union conference in Australia proved to be exactly what was needed for the world field. "My idea is that the General Conference Committee should leave the details of the affairs of America in the hands of the Union Conferences," he said at one session. "Our policy abroad has been feeble; it has been weak; it has not been in harmony with the great profession we have made. And we are having that reflex influence all through the United States." He also suggested replacing the term "foreign lands" with "missions."[35]

He spoke with authority on how one Australian Conference had covered too much territory—the five colonies of Australia, Tasmania, and Fiji. Ellen White's counsel, upon her arrival in Australia, was to divide into smaller conferences covering less territory. They had also merged the tract and missionary society, Sabbath School, and Religious Liberty Association under the umbrella of the conference committee and repeated the same pattern when they organized the Australasian Union in 1894. By the time of the 1901 General Conference session, the Australasian Union consisted of six conferences, with Tasmania and West Australia being General Conference missions.[36]

The large committee set up to reorganize the world field along these lines elected Daniells as chair, and at the close of the session, they also installed Daniells, now forty-two years old, as chair of the General Conference Committee. He did not assume the title of president of the General Conference until later, but he was effectively serving in that capacity after the 1901 General Conference session.[37]

One of the first things Daniells did upon assuming the presidency was to publicly proclaim the importance of the canvassing work. "This phase of our work is especially ordained of God for the world-wide proclamation of his last message to men," he said in an address in the Battle Creek College Chapel. "Canvassing for our literature affords an opportunity for hundreds to effectually make this

---

33 A. G. Daniells to Ellen G. White, October 4, 1900, Ellen G. White Estate.
34 *Advent Review and Sabbath Herald*, February 19, 1901, p. 128.
35 Ibid., April 30, 1901, p. 280.
36 General Conference Bulletin, April 7, 1901, p. 90; April 9, 1901, p. 162.
37 *Advent Review and Sabbath Herald*, May 14, 1901, p. 20.

truth known to the world. It is a means by which the following words of the psalmist are being fulfilled: 'The Lord gave the word: great was the company of those that published it' Ps. 68:11."[38]

He trumpeted the call for reviving Adventist literature evangelism, especially among the 20,000 Adventists in the Lake Union, of which he also became president for a time. "If we would take up this work in earnest, we could warn every man, woman, and child in this Union Conference in a short time," he predicted. "It could be done if our people would only work."[39]

His new job required lots of travel, and deskbound W. A. Spicer carefully handled the mail in his absence. He also found a valuable subordinate in W. W. Prescott.

One of the first issues he had to resolve was taking the title of president, as is indicated in a letter to Willie White. "I note what you say with reference to retaining the title of 'President of the General Conference.'… I was never in harmony with what I considered the radical positions taken by Brethren Jones and Prescott on this point; and if any other man had been selected as Chairman of the Committee, I would have expressed my views sooner than I did. Soon after we returned from Indianapolis, a question arose with reference to furnishing certain written statements to Railway Companies and to statisticians regarding the General Conference. We were brought to the point where we had to face the question of the official head of our organization. We could not name any person as Chairman of the General Conference, because the Conference was not in session. We could not very well substitute the General Conference Committee for the Conference itself. Brother Prescott tried to adjust the matter, but gave it up, and took the position that it would be better to retain the title of president.

"We looked the Testimony up on which he had based the idea that the title was not to be retained, and found that it did not teach this. We concluded that the instruction given in that Testimony was to the effect that the one man acting as president of the General Conference, was not to be cumbered with the details of the entire Conference. We saw that this arrangement for the division of the field into separate, distinct Union Conferences met the point. We also saw that the instruction aimed to the putting away of kingly, autocratic, arbitrary power, and that this sort of power could be exercised by the Chairman of the General Conference Committee, no matter what title he carried. We saw further that the title itself was retained in the Testimony all the way through, thus showing that it was not the disuse or the extinction of the title that as under consideration."[40]

He added that the state conferences were "fearfully run down." One such conference was the Lake Union Conference, which was in need of streamlining and reorganization. Daniells temporarily serving as president and made the changes he felt were necessary before looking for someone qualified enough for the job.

The land E. A. Sutherland and Percy Magan found for a new Battle Creek College campus pleased him. "The little town called Berrien Springs is one of the prettiest little rural towns to be found in the

---

38   *Supplement to Review and Herald,* May 21, 1901, p. 1.
39   Ibid., p. 4.
40   A. G. Daniells to Willie C. White, July 1, 1901.

country," he wrote to Willie White.[41]

In one letter to Ellen White, Daniells explained to her why he chose to communicate through Willie. "On account of your weakness and your many burdens I have refrained from troubling you, just as far as possible, with my correspondence. I have written my perplexities to Brother White, with the request that he place these matters before you just as far as he deemed wise. I have been glad to hear that since the spring has opened you have been improving in health, and that your strength is in a measure being restored."[42]

Less than two years after assuming the responsibilities of president of the General Conference, Daniells wrote a lengthy letter to Willie White, one of his closest friends, about his deepest convictions and concerns. "In your letter of May 7 you call my attention to a problem to which I have given a great deal of anxious thought since coming from Australia to the United States. What you say about it greatly stirs my heart," he continued. "I could scarcely restrain tears while reading your statements the first time. I have read them with studied care several times to be sure that I understood you. I will here quote the portion of your letter to which I refer. You say:—

"'During the last week many things have been presented to Mother regarding our danger as a people of entering largely into commercial enterprises and losing the spirit of the message. She fears that what she has written about food stores, restaurants, and treatment rooms will not be understood in the light in which it was written. She feels that our people do not yet understand their responsibility in all parts of the world, in all Conferences to make it their life-work to prepare for the Lord's coming and to enter into these enterprises as secondary to that great work: as auxiliaries, as a means of support and of education and of training, while always and continually the chief object of life is kept in mind. That object is the preparation of the world to meet the Lord, and the chief means, the preaching of the present truth. Mother has expressed many fears that an effort will be made to set on foot some great movement emanating from Battle Creek, dominated and directed by men living in Battle Creek, for the establishment of food stores and restaurants; and she fears that this will become a commercial enterprise, and that more would be lost through the influence of commercialism than will be gained through the feeble missionary efforts that will be connected with this enterprise.'"[43]

When he became president, Daniells inherited two difficult people with issues that had overwhelmed his predecessors, O. A. Olsen and George A. Irwin. John Harvey Kellogg had made the Battle Creek Sanitarium world famous, and Archibald R. Henry had developed the Review and Herald into one of the biggest and best publishing houses in Michigan. Both had worked their wonders contrary to Ellen White's counsel.

The burning of the Review and Herald publishing house in December 1902 furnished Daniells with the opportunity to follow Ellen White's directions and get out of Battle Creek, which effectively took care of Henry.

---

41 Ibid.
42 A. G. Daniells to Ellen White, June 2, 1902.
43 A. G. Daniells to Willie C. White, May 17, 1903.

But Ellen White had good reason to harbor a fear against commercialism and Kellogg's work. Successful businesspeople had exploited the commercial possibilities of the foods Kellogg developed for his patients in the Battle Creek Sanitarium. Charles W. Post became a multimillionaire in the 1890s and many others were imitating him. W. K. Kellogg would soon rival Post in dominating the breakfast food industry.

Daniells continued quoting Willie White's letter: "'Mother pleads that our brethren in different parts of the United States shall organize for medical missionary work and that the work in our Union Conferences may be directed by the men in the field whose chief interests are the promotion of the gospel and that this and every enterprise which has a commercial phase to it shall be operated as a missionary enterprise, from missionary motives, by men well trained in present truth who engage in business as a means of support, that they may do missionary work and as a means of gaining access to those in whose behalf the missionary effort is bestowed.

"'I sincerely hope that you and your fellow-laborers on the General Conference Committee will give this matter careful consideration and instead of giving this work a cold shoulder and leaving the medical men who have not yet recovered from the influences of centralization to mould it, that you will take hold with all your energy, zeal, and enthusiasm that it may be a blessing to the world and an honor to our God.

> "... this movement is not rising and broadening and increasing in power in the world at the rate it once did, and at the rate every intelligent believer has reason to expect it should."

"'... The great object for which Seventh-day Adventists have been raised up is to prepare the world for the Coming Christ; the chief means for doing this work is the preaching of present truth, or the third angel's message of Rev. 14:6-12; there is great danger that we shall be turned away from the chief means by which our work is to be done to lines of work and methods of working that can not of themselves accomplish the great object for which God has brought us into existence.'"[44]

Daniells had seen this very situation since taking the helm of the world church, and its implications staggered him. "This Brother White, is a grave problem," he continued in his letter. "It is not a theory. It is a condition which we now face. It has given me serious, anxious thought during the last two years.... I do not want to be a pessimist. I am not by nature. But it is impossible for me to shut my eyes to facts and conditions that are just as plain as day light."[45]

He saw a great gap between the kind of influence Seventh-day Adventists should have in the world and the true state of the church in 1903. "It is a fact that this movement under the third angel's message is to be a rising, broadening movement, growing in power and influence until the whole earth is stirred by it, and lightened with its glory.

---

44   Ibid.
45   Ibid.

"It is a fact that this movement is not rising and broadening and increasing in power in the world at the rate it once did, and at the rate every intelligent believer has reason to expect it should."[46]

To back up his assertion, Daniells pointed out that the General Conference had spent $1.5 million dollars in evangelical work during the past year, and he estimated that adding all money spent at the local level would bring the total amount of funds spent to more than $2 million.

"When we think of the number of persons this money employs, and the amount of talent, energy, and effort that have been put into this movement, we should certainly be justified in looking for very definite, substantial returns."[47]

All this dedicated work had brought 603 new church members throughout the world field, but the official figures showed a loss of 1,718 Sabbath-keepers in unorganized companies and 1,133 among isolated believers, a net loss of 2,245 Sabbbath-keepers during the past two years. "A further comparison of the reports for 1900 and 1902 show little increase in any features of our work. We have forty-three more ordained ministers, but fourteen less licensed preachers, and forty-three less licensed missionaries. With the number of Sabbath-keepers we have, the number of paid workers in the field, and money expended, and especially the power, nature and purpose of the message we have been raised up to give to the world, what a stir we should have made, and what additions to our believers and workers we should have recorded.

"Now what is the trouble?… During the first twenty-five years of our history as a people the ministers studied their Bibles for a knowledge of this [the third angel's] message. They searched for light as miners search for the precious metals. When they found a ray they gave it to the world with all the zeal and assurance of men who realized their high calling. They went from place to place in new fields with their Bibles, charts and literature, earnestly telling everybody the message. At our camp-meetings the charts were hung up and this message was proclaimed with great earnestness. In their church work they urged young men into the ministry, and all the people into missionary service. When schools were first started it was to fit the young men for ministers, and the young women for missionary society secretaries, and city Bible workers. And all the time the chief point kept before all was the proclamation of the third angel's message. Then our ministry grew in numbers, grace and power, and our numbers increased rapidly.

"But it is different now. The clear, clean-cut, distinctive and peculiar doctrines of the message are to a large measure dropped. Much of our preaching differs but little from the other churches. Our people hear more about the fine points of educational reform, medical and philanthropic work, the gospel of health, etc. etc., than they do about the third angel's message."[48]

Daniells agreed that these things had their place in the great work of preparing for the second coming, but he felt that they still represented a pitfall for the church. "But I tell you the truth when I declare that these features are fast becoming the whole thing. They are being pushed in a way that

---

46 Ibid.
47 Ibid.
48 Ibid.

eliminates, or obliterates, or drops out, the central, chief, great point of the message."[49]

And here Daniells came to a fear that would define his entire administration and shape for a century the approach of the Seventh-day Adventist church in proclaiming the three angels' messages.

"Take for instance the medical work," he continued. "Its journals are devoted entirely and exclusively to that phase. The message of which it is but a part, a feature, and arm, is scarcely recognized. The most of the public addresses at our camp-meetings, in our schools and churches are in praise of this feature. The physicians, nurses, students and helpers hear little else from one year's end to another. Is it any wonder that they forget the message, and that many give up the truth? I tell you nothing will keep the rank and file of our people with this message but the message itself. To my mind the continual praise and uplifting of medical and rational remedies, anatomy, physiology and hygiene, and the establishment and operation of health food factories and restaurants commercializes the third angel's message. It popularizes that phase, and infatuates our young people with it, so that the peculiar, unpopular features lose their meaning and beauty."[50]

Daniells acknowledged facing a serious challenge in capturing the imagination of the bright Adventist young people.

"The flower and culture of the denomination is being swung almost entirely into the various lines of the medical branch," he feared. "Scarcely any young men of education are entering our ministry. Few young women are taking up Bible work. And it is almost impossible to get bright, educated young people to enter the canvassing work

"… The medical department can present that work in glowing terms and can offer inducements that no conference can possibly offer," he continued. "Young people can become professional nurses in two and three years. While taking the course they can get board, lodging, and part, at least, of their clothes. When finished they can earn from ten to twenty dollars per week. Then they are sure of speedy employment. As a rule they can associate with the rich and influential. Even greater things are held out to those who can complete the medical course.

"What can a conference hold out to young men and women for the ministry, Bible work, and canvassing, compared to what they see in the medical lines! To enter these other lines means to choose the road of unpopularity, self-denial, and apparent uncertainty so far as support is concerned. In the early days when this way was made prominent, the sturdy young people of the denomination chose it. They would do so now if a strong united effort was made to show them the excellence of that way. This

> "Brother White, if this denomination rushes on in the direction it has gone during the last ten years for ten years more, we shall be wrecked. We shall have no ministry and we shall have no third angel's message."

---

49   Ibid.
50   Ibid.

ought to be done. But how shall it be done, and who will unite to do it.

"Brother White, if this denomination rushes on in the direction it has gone during the last ten years for ten years more, we shall be wrecked. We shall have no ministry and we shall have no third angel's message. Point to the ministers of the breadth and power who have entered the ministry during the last ten years," he challenged White. "Count them up. My acquaintance with the whole ministry enabled me to say that the young ministers are a third rate lot. With our ministry gone to seed, our message dropped, and secondary features popularized and pushed by the pick of our young people, where shall we land?"[51]

Daniells thus boiled over with passion to restore the ministry, Bible work, and canvassing to its proper dignity to prepare a people to stand in the day of the Lord.

"My heart burns," he concluded. "My soul is stirred to its depths. Some nights I lie awake in agony of mind over our situation. At times I am almost overwhelmed with discouragement. Then I gather courage and dedicate my whole being to the Lord to take hold of this work to call this people back onto the main line."[52]

Daniells faced many challenges early on in his presidency, but he steadily moved forward in the work he felt God had called him to do. In July of 1903 he wrote to Ellen White about the good response of the local congregation to the Spirit of Prophecy testimonies on moving headquarters. The brethren had chartered two furniture cars, which were expected to leave Battle Creek on Wednesday, August 5 and arrive on Monday, August 10 in Washington, D.C., the exact place she said the church should move its headquarters to.[53]

With the encouragement of Ellen White, Daniells also successfully prevented Kellogg from gaining too much power. "I have lost all hope of Dr. Kellogg," she wrote to him. "He is, I fully believe, past the day of his reprieve. I have not written him a line for about one year. I am instructed not to write to him.

"I have been reading over the matter given me for him, and the light is that we must call our people to a decision. God calls for every jot and tittle of influence to be placed on the side of truth and righteousness."[54]

Neglected Fields

Daniells had tremendous world vision, but Ellen White reminded him of two great needy fields in North America: the South and the major metropolitan areas.

"You bring up the far-off mission fields, great London and the neglected fields further away," she wrote to him. "We stand rebuked by God because the large cities right within our sight are unworked and unwarned. A terrible charge of neglect is brought against those who have been long in the work,

---

51 Ibid.
52 Ibid.
53 A. G. Daniells to Ellen G. White, July 27, 1903.
54 Ellen G. White to A. G. Daniells, December 16, 1905.

in this very America, and yet have not entered the large cities. What has been done in Philadelphia, in New Orleans, in St. Louis, and in other cities that I might name? We have done none too much for foreign fields, but we have done comparatively nothing for the great cities right beside our own.

"You speak of the work which should be done in America, but which is undone… I wish to speak, not merely in behalf of the Southern field, but in behalf of the large cities, whose neglected, unwarned condition is a condemnation to our people, who claim to be missionaries for the Master.

"There is the great city of New York. Much might have been done in it that has not been done… We have scarcely touched Greater New York with the tips of our fingers."

"The very men held in Battle Creek, where the Lord has said that they should not be held, could have entered these cities, and under the guidance of wise leaders, whether ministers or laymen, a successful effort might have been carried forward."[55]

"I have received a copy of a letter written by Elder Haskell to Elder Daniells, telling about the work in New York," she wrote to him soon after he took charge. "I am desirous that you shall both visit New York City, and investigate the matter of buying the hall about which Brother Haskell speaks.

"Go to New York City. Look the ground over carefully, and see whether it is advisable to purchase the hall and the land on which it stands. Perhaps the land could be leased for a term of years. I have instructed that some such methods will have to be followed in the work in the large cities. If after careful consideration, you decide that it is best to purchase the hall, we shall do all in our power to raise the money. But it is best to move understandingly. Pray, pray, pray, for if possible Satan will close the doors which have opened for the entrance of truth. The Lord desires a center for the truth to be established in the great, wicked city of New York.

"I ask you to investigate the work in New York, and lay plans for establishing a memorial for God in this city. It is to be a center for missionary effort and in it a Sanitarium is to be established.

"The work in the cities of the South is to be advanced, but the work in the city of New York is now the important interest."[56]

Daniells appeared to listen to her counsel to a certain degree, but Ellen White also counseled him to not succumb to power. "Let us be careful how we press our opinions upon those whom God has instructed … Brother Daniells, God would not have you suppose that you can exercise a kingly power over your brethren."[57] In spite of all this, it was clear that he approached city evangelism through tracts.

"When Brother White was with me in Battle Creek last November I received a number of letters from you containing instruction regarding the work in the Southern field," Daniells wrote to her. "Brother White can tell you how he and I spent a large portion of one day reading these communications together, talking over various points, and praying for understanding.

"While I could not understand all that was written I could understand enough to help me to change in some things, and to place me on my guard concerning others. I have read what you have

---

55   Ibid.
56   Ibid., October 28, 1901.
57   Ibid., April 12, 1903.

written many times, and have earnestly prayed for help to do my whole duty."

"You will be glad to know that nearly a million tracts have been taken by our people since Christmas. And the orders are still rolling in."[58]

She also spoke of the importance of medical missionary work, recalling how the Lord had impressed her with the importance of temperance and that the church should have a sanitarium to help the sick. She noted that through this means they would reach all classes of people. "Medical missionary work, ministering to the sick and suffering, cannot be separated from the gospel," she said.[59]

When it came to medical missionary work, Daniells said all the right things and tried to follow Ellen White's counsel, even if his heart was drawn more toward the publishing work. A committee on plans acknowledged true medical missionary work as part of the gospel and recommended this branch be made part of the conference organization at the General Conference session of 1905. One resolution recommended "that the medical missionary work in all its features receive the same fostering care and financial support from the conference organization, churches, and people that are given to other branches of our work." In clarifying it, Daniells said that medical workers would be treated as other workers with the exception that in some cases they would be able to sustain themselves.[60]

He organized a Medical Department of the General Conference with two designated physicians: W. A. Ruble to help the sanitariums, and D. H. Kress to present the Adventist health message in public meetings within and without the church. The General Conference Committee also financially assisted new schools at Loma Linda, California, and Madison, Tennessee, both at the behest of Ellen White.

In a letter to Kellogg, Daniells wrote, "I can assure you, Doctor, that what little I am able to do for the advancement of the medical work is done from my heart; for I believe that is just as much my work as in any other phase of gospel work."[61]

In spite of all these statements about the medical work, his actual programs left out medical workers and stressed the gospel ministry. A public announcement reveals this attitude. After the 1905 General Conference session, he brought in his predecessor, G. A. Irwin, from the Australasian Division as a general vice president so Daniells could devote more of his time to "the great problems of our mission fields, the translation, production, and distribution of literature in behalf of the great masses of humanity now in the darkness of heathenism, the improvement and enlargement of our ministry, the development of our educational work, and the visiting of distant mission fields."[62]

Furthermore, Daniells dealings with the infancy of Loma Linda seemed to speak to his hesitancy to support the medical work. In 1905 John Burden, a Pacific Coast Adventist minister, found a bankrupt resort for sale at Loma Linda, California, and Ellen White told him to negotiate for it. She had seen the place in vision.

---

58   A. G. Daniells to Ellen G. White, February 24, 1903, Ellen G. White Estate.
59   General Conference Bulletin, April 12, 1901, pp. 202–205.
60   General Conference Bulletin, June 1, 1905, p. 8.
61   A. G. Daniells to John Harvey Kellogg, April 4, 1902.
62   *Advent Review and Sabbath Herald,* August 3, 1905, p. 6.

Burden immediately started raising money, but the local conference, after consulting with the General Conference in Washington, was told to not get involved.

Was Daniells supportive of Ellen White's counsel? Or did he fear that a glamorous medical center at Loma Linda would lure bright young people away from the ministry? Needless to say, the $38,900 needed to purchase Loma Linda was raised in seven months from private, not conference, sources.[63]

It certainly appeared that Daniells was not supportive of the medical work and that he preferred to focus his attention on publishing. When examining ways to reach the many foreign-born immigrants moving to places like New York City, he established a book depository and encouraged "the circulation of foreign literature among the millions of other tongues of the great Eastern cities."[64]

In addition to his idea of a book depository, the following missionary campaign came out of the 1905 General Conference session as a recommendation of how to share the three angels message with people in North America.

- Place the *Review and Herald* in every Sabbath-keeping home.
- Start a general campaign in North America for the circulation of missionary periodicals.
- Have the conference interest the church members in the sale of Adventist books.
- Arouse interest in Adventism by the liberal use of message-filled tracts, securing subscriptions for Adventist periodicals, holding Bible readings and cottage meetings, and engaging in missionary correspondence.[65]

It was voted that the primary method for sharing the gospel would be through literature circulation, publishing "four special numbers of *The Signs of the Times* and the *Watchman*, two special issues of *Life and Health*, and such issues of the foreign papers as the publishers may deem best."[66]

All the while Ellen White prodded him to get big city evangelism going. His burden for the world field was wonderful, but the big cities and the South had been neglected for too long.

At the 1909 General Conference session, he once again pointed out pitfalls facing the medical work. "One danger is that our evangelical laborers are apt to become so busy in other lines as to neglect the medical work; while the second danger is that our medical men may become so interested in medical work as to forget the foreign missionary work and other phases of the message....

"The hour has come for this message to be proclaimed to mankind, and this mighty truth is to-day operating upon the hearts of men," Daniells proclaimed. "And when that message comes to men, and they give it a respectful attention, it lays hold upon them with a grip that they can scarcely break.

"The point I wish to call your attention to is the position to which we have now come. Where are we to-night in this message? Sixty-five years it has been sounding. The message was to be finished in a

---

63 The Vision Bold: An Illustrated History of the Seventh-day Adventist Philosophy of Health, eds. Warren L. Johns and Richard H. Utt (Washington, D.C.: Review and Herald Publishing Association, 1977), p. 176.
64 Ibid., June 1, 1905, p. 24.
65 Ibid., June 8, 1905, p. 30.
66 Ibid.

single generation. Where is it to go?—It is to go to all the world, to every kindred, tongue, and people."[67]

And how was this to be done? Ellen White appealed powerfully for city evangelism at the 1909 General Conference session. "When I think of the many cities still unwarned, I cannot rest," she said after eight years of pleading for big city evangelism to be started. "It is distressing to think that they have been neglected so long …"[68]

Ellen White finally lost patience with Daniells in 1910 presumably over his failure to initiate city evangelism and refused to see him when he showed up to visit her at Elmshaven. She had given him plenty of instruction and wanted him to rally the entire denomination behind big city evangelism.

"I was sorry I could not have talked with you while at St. Helena, concerning the work for our cities," a disappointed Daniells wrote to Ellen White. "I wanted to tell you that I shall take hold of this work with all my heart … I have felt greatly concerned about this for several months, and now I feel that I must take hold of this work personally. Whatever money or laborers may be required in these places, I will do my best to secure. I am willing to spend months in personal efforts with the workers, if necessary."[69]

He returned to his office, cancelled a trip to Australia and a summer camp meeting itinerary, and organized a major seminar on big city evangelism as part of the 1910 Autumn Council.[70] Several prominent church members presented papers as the basis of a study to work the cities. Daniells led off the meeting, stating the importance of this work. C. H. Edwards pointed out the need for reaching the larges masses of foreign people crowding into the Eastern cities, the best way by Bible and literature workers. R. D. Quinn and O. O. Bernstein spoke on the importance of public evangelism. Drs. D. H. Kress and David Paulson presented papers on medical evangelistic work. Other topics were the role of literature and funding for city work.

A Committee on City Work went over all the proposals and made several specific recommendations, including:

That the strong Western conferences financially assist the weaker Eastern conferences where the big cities were located, where reaching the multitudes were beyond their resources.

That the missionary idea be kept before students in the sanitariums and encourage that graduates of programs such as nursing be encouraged to work at training centers in the cities.

The major recommendation was that "medical and evangelistic efforts should be more closely combined."[71] It was also recommended that a city mission be headed by a minister, a physician, and their wives—the ministerial and health work were to go hand in hand.

---

67 General Conference Bulletin, May 17, 1909, p. 40.
68 Howard B. Weeks, *Adventist Evangelism in the Twentieth Century* (Washington, D.C.: Review and Herald Publishing Association, 1969), p. 27.
69 A. G. Daniells to Ellen G. White, May 26, 1910; Weeks, *Adventist Evangelism in the Twentieth Century*, p. 38.
70 Weeks, *Adventist Evangelism in the Twentieth Century*, pp. 38, 39.
71 General Conference Committee minutes, November 23–30, 1910.

In spite of all this work, Daniells shelved the proposals or the General Conference Committee took no official action upon them, because nothing happened in regards to city evangelism. Instead, he devoted himself to overseas missions and upgrading the Adventist ministry, starting with ministerial institutes. The first one was held in 1911 in Knoxville, Tennessee, for all ministers, conference presidents, and Bible workers in the Southern states—it did not include physicians or nurses. W. W. Prescott spoke on doctrinal themes, and G. B. Starr presented a series of studies on the Holy Spirit.

An institute in Philadelphia, Pennsylvania, for conference workers in the Atlantic, Columbia, and Canadian Unions resulted in a great revival. Other institutes followed at Walla Walla, Battle Creek, Los Angeles, and Stanborough Park near London. "In each case there was a repetition of the notable conversion experience among the ministers present … a reconsecration of the ministry in its new-found evangelical unity was the most remarkable result of the meetings," wrote Howard Weeks in his chronicle of Adventist evangelism during the twentieth century.[72]

The institutes resulted in remarkable unity among Adventist preachers. Unfortunately, they gave very little instruction on how to impact the general public, and there was no talk of medical missionary work or the need for ministers and physicians to work together, as is seen in the topics covered.

- What Constitutes the Christian Ministry?
- The Place of the Ministry in the Gospel Plan
- The Call to the Ministry
- The Holy Spirit's Place in the Gospel Ministry
- Evangelistic Work of the Minister in New Fields
- Pastoral Work or the Minister With the Church
- The Minister in His Study
- Preparation and Delivery of the Sermon
- The Improvement of the Vocabulary

Daniells did include medical missionary work on the agenda at a 1912 council on city evangelistic work that was held in Takoma Park, Maryland, but it was mixed in among other topics such as advertising, the scriptures, visiting, Bible workers, magazine sellers, the press, preaching, and the workers. The council agreed that the real mission of the Adventist evangelist was to present the teachings of the Bible. At the meeting J. H. N. Tindall and C. W. Garnsey advocated for health evangelism. Tindall recommended "the affiliation of a qualified physician and nurse with evangelistic campaigns so that sick persons might actually be visited and that men might be brought to see a certain unity and wholeness in an evangelistic message that embraced not only personal salvation but also physical health."

The council also adopted a resolution urging that "the medical missionary work in all its phases … be made more prominent in our evangelistic work than it has in the past." It recommended that ministers prepare themselves to give health lectures and to secure charts and other equipment for the purpose and reserve one night a week for health and temperance questions. It also encouraged ministers

---

72 Weeks, *Adventist Evangelism in the Twentieth Century*, p. 51.

to visit the sick and to help them.[73]

But the medical work, the right arm of the church, still struggled to become integrated into the evangelistic ministry of the church. In 1913 it was once again urged that the medical work take a prominent role in evangelism.

"Years of endeavor have been put forth in the effort to bring about a union between the workers in different lines, but without the desired result," reads one official account of a General Conference meeting. "We are living in the last days. The end of all things is at hand. The gospel message must be given in this generation, and the work is delayed so long as there is a lack of interest in any phase of the work.

"There must be a combination of evangelical and medical work. This combination was manifested in the life of Jesus Christ, and must be in the lives of his representatives. A union of interests must be seen and felt before the work can be finished. Dr. D. H. Kress and Elder B. G. Starr in their remarks emphasized the importance of this unity."[74]

Daniells apparently gave only lip service to these proposals and devoted his dynamic leadership style to promote evangelism and develop evangelistic talent. By 1913 fifteen evangelists worked the Greater New York area. Others included J. W. McCord in San Francisco; K. C. Russell in Chicago; Drs. David Paulson and D. H. and Lauretta Kress in Chicago; Charles T. Everson in Chicago; J. S. Washburn in Philadelphia; and Gustavus P. Rodgers in Baltimore. Carlyle B. Haynes used public relations so effectively in a 1911 Baltimore campaign that his new-convert press agent, a newspaperman named Walter L. Burgan, became head of the first public relations bureau in the General Conference office.[75]

Adventist evangelism made such great strides with Daniells leading the way that the medical work may have seemed unnecessary. And with the decline of the Ottoman Turkish Empire, many Adventists believed that Armageddon was right around the corner, especially after Turkey joined forces with Germany in World War I.

With all that was going on in the world, Daniells didn't need physicians and the health message to help attract an audience. "Turkey, Daniells wrote, fulfilled the specifications of that power described in prophecy as the 'king of the north,' and according to the prophecy would ultimately lose all its possessions in Africa and Europe, be driven out of Europe, re-establish a capital in Jerusalem, and then finally be permanently obliterated, receiving no help from any allies. Thereupon, Elder Daniells concluded, would be launched the battle of Armageddon, bringing the close of human history and the return of Christ as seen in other prophecies."[76]

The Height of Evangelism

The start of World War I fueled a revival some people thought had begun with Ellen White's powerful appeals for city evangelism at the 1909 General Conference, and Daniells stood at the forefront of

---

73   Ibid., pp. 51–59.
74   General Conference Bulletin, May 20, 1913, p. 63.
75   Weeks, *Adventist Evangelism in the Twentieth Century*, pp. 51–69.
76   Ibid., p. 78.

it. Newspaper reporters besieged him for interviews. His big break came at a series of public meetings he agreed to conduct in Portland, Maine.

His opening night meeting attracted a crowd of 2,000 people, followed by an invitation to repeat his lecture to the Portland Business Men's Club.

"Well, I did not know that I could ever stand before 2,250 of the first business and professional men of a city and talk our message as I did in that club room," he wrote to I. H. Evans. "The mayor sat directly in front of me and the editor of the evening press by my side and never took their eyes from me the whole time. A divine power was present. At the close, many came and thanked me most cordially for the address. Some said it was the first serious and definite explanation they had ever heard of the present terrible struggle.

"I have felt very solemn all day—almost sad as I have thought of those upturned faces. I wonder if there is not some way to get before this class of men in our cities … We had nearly 2,000 people out Sunday night, and only a few of them were our own people. There is something more than ordinary about this whole work in Portland. I am seeking the Lord with all my heart to know how to do my part."

His meetings continued with standing-room-only crowds—hundreds were turned away at one service.

The Portland Daily Eastern Argus commented on February 21, 1915, "A half hour before Dr. Daniells began his lecture and every available seat was taken in the great amphitheater. Hundreds stood on the main floor and also in both balconies. More than a thousand were turned away, the police taking precautions that no more forced their way through the entrances. Great enthusiasm prevailed as the various scenes of the war were thrown on the screen, and though the lecture lasted an hour and a half, the great throng gave excellent attention throughout."[77]

Was Daniells fulfilling Ellen White's request to reach the cities? He may have thought so: "We believe that the experience of the last few weeks in Portland will be duplicated in many cities," he said. "The people are anxious to know the meaning of the great world events. The prophecies of the Word furnish answers to their eager inquiries. Seventh-day Adventists, who have the light of prophecy, should realize that God has called them to the places they occupy, for such a time as this. Never in my experience had I witnessed such a desire on the part of the public to hear the message we are proclaiming to the world. We are deeply impressed that we are entering upon a new experience in our work in behalf of the masses in the cities."[78]

Daniells repeated this success in Pittsburgh, packing the 2,500-seat Pitt Theater. He then moved on to Minneapolis, Duluth, and St. Paul in Minnesota; Columbus, Ohio; and Superior Wisconsin, among other cities. Evangelists E. L. Cardey and Charles T. Everson enjoyed similar successes in New York City.[79]

While enjoying a smashing success in evangelism, Daniells did not financially support the

---

77 Ibid., p. 88.
78 Ibid., pp. 85–89.
79 Ibid., pp. 78–93.

struggling College of Medical Evangelists, which was in desperate need of a teaching hospital in Los Angeles that was owned and controlled by the school to satisfy accreditation requirements of the American Medical Association. The 1915 Fall Council, approving the medical school upgrade, appropriated no money for this purpose but turned the fund-raising over to a volunteer effort of dedicated women led by Mrs. S. N. Haskell. Unfortunately, they failed to secure the needed amount during the next year.

At this time, the Adventist ministry seemed to have little need for a medical school, and at the 1916 Fall Council the matter was dropped and plans were passed for evangelism, calling for two strong companies in North America, including a leader, singer, publicity agent, two or more Bible workers, and others, such as musicians, nurses, colporteurs, etc.—maybe physicians fell under the category of "others."

> "I believe still today, to the very depths of my heart, that this is the closing message of God; that this is the last call to humanity; that this is the generation for the finishing of that call, and that it will be finished in our day."

The General Conference finally appropriated $30,000 for this purpose at the 1917 Fall Council provided that Magan could first come up with the same amount needed to start hospital construction.

A 1917 survey revealed that during 1916 major evangelistic campaigns had been conducted in more than half of the 71 cities in the United States with a population of 100,000 or more. Adventist evangelists planned to cover the other half.

The second coming of Jesus had never seemed more imminent.

"Whose heart has not been cheered by the experiences of our city evangelists the last two or three years?" Daniells said. "During the past winter the largest buildings our evangelists have been able to pay for in a number of cities have been well filled, and at times thousands of anxious people have been unable to get seats or standing room. The authorities have been compelled to lock the doors to prevent overcrowding. This has been the experience of our evangelists in New York City, Philadelphia, Detroit, Atlanta, Nashville and other cities. Not only have thousands come to hear, but they have become deeply interested and have continued to come week after week… Hundreds have taken their stand for the truth and are now members of our churches… It looks as if we must secure larger halls, and organize stronger staffs of helpers."[80]

He seemed to be finally fulfilling Ellen White's calls for a larger proclamation of the message. "We are all acquainted with the stirring messages that came to us through the Spirit of Prophecy a few years ago in behalf of the masses gathered in our large cities. When these messages began coming, we had

---

80   Ibid., p. 97.

done but little really successful work in these great, congested centers. We did not know how to make ourselves known or heard. The task seemed insurmountable. These cities seemed like so many mighty Jerichos whose walls we could neither scale nor throw down. But aroused by oft-repeated and most urgent messages, we applied ourselves to the great undertaking. Our efforts have been blessed of God … We are getting inside the ramparts, and today the outlook is good."[81]

Daniells reached high tide in 1918, and the General Conference session that year started a long tradition of meeting in major cities, starting with San Francisco. Adventists on any continent could easily travel there.

"I believe this is the last generation of men who shall live on this earth," he proclaimed to a Sabbath assembly. "I believe still today, to the very depths of my heart, that this is the closing message of God; that this is the last call to humanity; that this is the generation for the finishing of that call, and that it will be finished in our day."[82]

A clean-cut, clear message; a literature expressing that message; a responsive, disciplined organization of people sharing that message; and a mighty infilling of the Holy Spirit added up to a global impact during the horrors of a world war seeming at times like an apocalypse. The movement he had taken over and developed beyond the founders' wildest dreams had what it took to reach the 300 million people in India and China with its population of 400 million, not to mention the entire world population.[83]

But while extending Adventism around the world, Daniells continued to give low priority to accrediting the College of Medical Evangelists. On August 4, 1921, Percy Magan summed up the difficulty of working with his General Conference superiors in a letter to his friend and benefactor Lida Funk Scott. An American Medical Association delegation had just issued a report of changes needed in order to grant the school full grade A status.

"We had a pretty strenuous time together for a while—Dr. Thomason, Dr. Evans and myself on one side; Elders Daniells, Knox and Mr. Bowen on the other," Magan wrote. "It reminded me of some of the meetings which Dr. Sutherland and I used to have with Elder Daniells in the early years of this century over the whole medical question; and also a bit later on when we first went to Tennessee. At first these men were not inclined to do anything at all looking toward meeting the requirements of the American Medical Association. However, their position in this was soon made to appear so utterly untenable that they are willing now to sit down quietly with us somewhere along the first of the year and discuss the whole matter. I feel that it will take an immense amount of the great and good wisdom of the good God to be by with them as far as the school is concerned …

"We have been told in the Spirit of Prophecy that we must work in harmony with 'the legal requirements of the State and nation in the matter of training our young physicians.' It seems very difficult for these men to get this matter clear in their minds …

---

81   Ibid., pp. 95, 96.
82   General Conference Bulletin, April 1, 1918, p. 9.
83   Ibid.

"They do not see what business the American Medical Association has to dictate to us concerning medical education. They want to run everything their own way from Washington just as they please, and this, as I understand it, the Council on Medical Education will not tolerate. One thing certain—if they refuse to do the thing which the Council on Medical Education and Hospitals of the American Medical Association request them to do, the school will be closed, for the American Medical Association will simply shove it down into the 'C' grade—then these brethren will be in a place where they will have to explain to the people that they have caused the closing of the school because of their determination not to allow the physicians to have anything to say to the financial management; not to permit the headquarters of the school to be in Los Angeles, and not to agree to having an executive committee with reasonable powers. They are going to be in a mighty hard place when they go up against this proposition, because Seventh-day Adventists do have executive committees, and many of our college presidents are also the business managers of the institutions over which they preside, and I don't believe that these leading brethren will ever be able to face the storm of criticism that they will be bound to meet if they force a situation which will mean the closing of the school."[84]

Daniells ultimately complied with state standards, but his heart remained with developing a powerful, spirit-filled gospel ministry.

Daniells kept the Adventist ministry at the forefront of bringing the church militant to its climax, both as president until 1922 and then as executive secretary. He helped found *Ministry Magazine* as a valuable ministerial tool. His inspired training institutes developed into an advanced Bible school at Pacific Union College and ultimately the SDA Theological Seminary, originally near General Conference headquarters and now at Berrien Springs, Michigan. Several larger-than-life Adventist ministers came out of the Daniells administration: Charles T. Everson, one of the first Adventist city evangelists; Roy Allen Anderson, a native of Australia, distinguished theologian, and longtime editor of *Ministry Magazine*; Leroy Edwin Froom, author of scholarly books on the faith of our fathers; Francis David Nichol, prominent writer and longtime editor of the *Review*, and perhaps the most famous, H. M. S. Richards, founder of the *Voice of Prophecy* radio broadcast and one of the greatest Adventist preachers of all time.

But the passage of 100 years would show that taking the gospel of the kingdom to all the world as a witness unto all nations needed more than money, organization, and educated, high-powered ministers, canvassers, and Bible workers.

---

84 Letter, Percy T. Magan to Lida Funk Scott, September 4, 1921, Magan Collection, Center for Adventist Research, Andrews University, Berrien Springs, Michigan.

A Profile of Percy T. Magan:

A Ministry Built Around Ellen White

The life of Percy Magan always reminded his friends of the nineteenth century Horatio Alger success stories dramatizing the rise of poor boys to fame and fortune through hard work, temperance, and thrift. His elevation to the highest councils of the American Medical Association was indeed impressive, especially when one considers that following Ellen White brought him onto a first-name basis with the top scientists of the Mayo Clinic and turned her perplexity about how to fund a Grade A medical school at Loma Linda into reality.

Magan was born on November 13, 1867, at Marlfield House near Gorey, County of Wexford, Ireland. His grandfather, a Protestant named George Magan, married an O'Conner, a Catholic descendant of the last king of Ireland, Roderick O'Connor. His father, another Percy Magan, owned a large estate, and Percy Tilson Magan would have inherited great wealth had he turned down Adventism.[1]

His education began at the age of nine at Arnold House in London and later St. George's School at Huntingdon.[2] Not wanting a military or church career, sixteen-year-old Magan had trouble pleasing his father. "He [his father] discouraged the lad by repeating that he would never amount to anything, and that he was a disgrace to the family," Lillian Magan, second wife to Percy Magan, recalled years later in an interview.

---

1   Interview with Dr. Lillian Magan, on file at the Heritage House on the old Madison College Campus, Madison, Tennessee.
2   Edward A. Sutherland, M.D., "My Sixty Years' Friendship with Percy T. Magan," *The Journal, Alumni Association College of Medical Evangelists*, March 1948.

About this time, the senior Magan met an Irishman in Dublin looking for people to work on a small farm he owned in Nebraska. He offered to make a great cattleman of young Percy in two years for the sum of $650—room and board were part of the deal.

He thus bade farewell to his four sisters and younger brother and started his legend as a teenager facing the new world all alone with $64 in his pocket under contract to a stranger in an unknown, dreary land. After arriving in Red Cloud, Nebraska, he immediately developed a dislike for ranching. But it was while he was living on the ranch that friends in the community invited him to attend an Adventist evangelistic meeting, and the message captivated him. Soon after hearing the good news, he decided to be baptized into the Seventh-day Adventist faith even though his father threatened to disinherit him.

Like many new converts, he became more Adventist than the Adventists, and his name soon appeared in the *Review and Herald*, whose readers would become familiar with him in the years to come.

The March 23, 1887, issue of the *Review* carried an announcement of a special course training Bible workers in the Nebraska Conference. Those wanting to come were urged to send their names to nineteen-year-old Magan in Lincoln.[3] An article later in the year reported young Magan and a Brother Harr conducting successful meetings near Grand Island, Nebraska.[4]

Years later, he described his initial Adventist experience to his close friend Edward A. Sutherland. "In the summer of 1887 I was 'tent master' of a company which took up work at Cambridge, Nebraska. Elders L.A. Hoopes and J.E. Jayne were the preachers and Eliza Burleigh was the organist. In the end a bad wind storm tore the tent to pieces. Elders Hoopes and Jayne went off to their homes and I remained holding Bible studies and making an attempt at preaching in sod houses in that part of southern Nebraska and northern Kansas. Then I received orders to pack the remains of the tent and what other equipment we had and send it to Grand Island, Nebraska. This I did. I landed in Grand Island one evening with exactly ten cents in my pocket. The camp meeting was held there and after the camp meeting I was assigned to work with Elder Daniel Nettleton. He followed the interest which had been generated by the camp meeting and a man by the name of Harr and I were supposed to work in the country around about. He left and went to the General Conference at Oakland and I was left alone. I worked until the following January, traveling about afoot in the snow, sleeping at any farm house where night happened to find me, holding Bible readings and preaching in school houses.

"For several years I had terrible coughs in the winter and it was the consensus of opinion that I had tuberculosis or 'consumption' as it was called in those days. You will remember that the bacillus of tuberculosis had not yet been discovered yet and Pasteur's work was in its infancy. At any rate I wasn't in the best of health and at a 'worker's meeting' held in Lincoln, Nebraska, it was voted that Elizabeth Yale, Fred Hebbard, and I should go to Battle Creek. Miss Yale and Mr. Hebbard were quitting the work of the conference to get more schooling at the Battle Creek College and I was given a leave of absence because of my health. I had a little pay coming to me which paid my fare to Battle Creek and I went to work in the Battle Creek Sanitarium five hours a day for my board, room and treatment. I

---

3   *The Review and Herald*, March 23, 1887, p. 192.
4   Ibid., November 22, 1887, p. 733.

began to mend and entered the school of nursing, in the third class I think that the denomination ever conducted. I became acquainted with Ida Rankin and she became interested in me and got old Brother Reuben Wright to pay for my schooling. You will remember in those days it cost $140 for board, room and tuition per annum. I entered the school in April, 1888, which left me only a couple of months of the school session. I worked during the summer nursing in the Battle Creek Sanitarium where I earned $15 a month and my board and room and in the fall of 1888 I reentered the school, rooming with you, as you will recall, in the old west hall. I stayed practically to the end of the year, and Reuben Wright paid the bill."[5]

Rooming with Sutherland at Battle Creek College during the 1888-89 school year began a nearly sixty-year friendship impacting the entire Seventh-day Adventist denomination. Magan was apparently the more religious of the two at the outset.

In 1888, he accepted what Ellen White, A. T. Jones and E. G. Waggoner taught on the issue of righteousness by faith, while other prominent denominational workers like Uriah Smith, George I. Butler, president of the General Conference, and W. W. Prescott turned it down. Magan later led Sutherland to accept the same message in the summer of 1891 at a teacher's institute near Petosky, Michigan.[6]

"Percy had some advantage over me," Sutherland wrote sixty years later. "He was enjoying the religious experience of one thoroughly converted. He accepted the promises of the Bible and the righteousness of Christ without question. My faith was too weak for me to accept personally God's promises concerning the gift of His righteousness. Percy realized that I was endeavoring to obtain righteousness by works, and he skillfully worked with me until he brought me where I fully accepted God's promises. For this I felt I owed him everything."[7]

Magan took righteousness by faith to its highest levels.

First Major Assignment

Magan launched his denominational career as an assistant to Elder S. N. Haskell on a round-the-world trip to evaluate Adventist overseas missions. Young Magan chronicled their journey in a series of *Review* articles and would be known to *Review* readers from then on through the rest of his life.

His first dispatch from China and Japan lamented that only one Adventist, Abram LaRue, worked as a colporteur selling books in these two populous countries.

He felt the Chinese could appreciate the third angel's message. "They are naturally a very industrious people," he commented. "Almost all the tea consumed in the United States and in Europe is

---

5   Percy Magan to E. A. Sutherland, July 23, 1937, Center for Adventist Research, Andrews University, Berrien Springs, Michigan.
6   Chronological arrangement of events in the life of Percy Tilson Magan and those associated with him, as told by Edward A. Sutherland, Center for Adventist Research, Andrews University, Berrien Springs, Michigan.
7   Edward A. Sutherland, M.D., "My Sixty Years' Friendship with Percy T. Magan," *The Journal, Alumni Association College of Medical Evangelists*, March 1948.

produced by China…. Here is an opportunity for faithful missionaries to labor among these homes."[8]

Japan also impressed him as being open to Adventism in that Brother LaRue had sold more than $40 worth of publications there in eight days. He concluded with a great world vision, "The third angel's message has already been carried to Europe, and beyond to Siberia, and its rays have gladdened the hearts of many in the islands of the seas. But this message must be pushed farther; these countries must be reached. The Macedonian cry comes from them as well as from others. The fields are white, ready for the harvest. It is high time that some were fitting themselves to enter these fields. The Lord in his mercy has gone before and opened the way."[9]

> "It is an admitted fact, by all who have ever made a study of the subject, that no one can have such an influence among the heathen as the Christian physician."

The next report of the Magan-Haskell odyssey came from Cape Colony, South Africa. He took a special interest of the Malaysian descendants of slaves imported there 200 years before and felt it remarkable that they had preserved their own culture despite the advances of civilization. Adventism had a few things in common with them in that they refused to drink alcoholic beverages or eat pork. Yet they closed their minds to Christianity, and Magan did not know how to approach them.

"It will need consecrated effort to carry the truth to them, and those who do take up the cross will need the wisdom of the serpent and the harmlessness of the dove."[10]

This trip, indeed, widened his horizons. "As we travel over the Master's vineyard, it seems a large field, and there is much yet to be done. At every place laborers are needed; the harvest is white, but the laborers are indeed few. It is time for us to awaken out of sleep, and make more strenuous efforts to tell these precious souls for whom the Saviour died, that soon he will return to earth to claim his own."[11]

Magan's writings from his journey with Haskell earned him a position as an editorial contributor to *The Youth's Instructor*.[12]

The political as well as religious situation of India confirmed his faith in the last day message of Adventism as well as the need for overseas missionary work. He saw the seeds of war in the rise of the great Russian and British empires, all coming to a head over the decline of the Ottoman Turks and the resulting fate of Constantinople.

"These things are only another sign of the end, and of the near coming of our Lord and Saviour Jesus Christ; as such they should be viewed, and efforts put forth by the people of God to

---

8   *Advent Review and Sabbath Herald*, September 3, 1889, p. 550.
9   Ibid., p. 551.
10   Ibid., November 26, 1889, p. 742.
11   Ibid.
12   Ibid., December 10, 1889, p. 784.

spread the glad tidings of the return of the world's Redeemer, ere the night cometh when no man can work."[13]

He saw a great need for skilled medical missionary work in approaching the millions in India and China. "It is an admitted fact, by all who have ever made a study of the subject, that no one can have such an influence among the heathen as the Christian physician."[14] As an example, he told the story of how a dedicated young Scottish physician opened up a native state in India to Christianity through the healing arts of medicine.

Magan received an urgent summons home once they landed in Australia, so he left Haskell and arrived at San Francisco in time to help dedicate the "Pitcairn," the first Adventist missionary ship, at a Bay Area camp meeting.

Haskell later reported that the trip cost $2,209.85 and that on the East Coast of Africa "Brother Magan was sick, and we prayed for him and he got better."[15]

He devoted the next several years to teaching Bible and history at Battle Creek College and writing articles for the *Review*, and in 1891 he was granted a ministerial license along with W. A. Spicer.

His *Review* articles revealed a profound belief in Adventism. In addition to his teaching duties, he visited churches to promote the educational work of the church, gave history lectures to a General Conference Bible school, and wrote a series of articles on the French Revolution, showing similarities between the time of trouble and the Reign of Terror.

"In all the articles which have preceded this one, I have endeavored to show, both from the Scriptures and from history, 'where we are, and whither we are tending,'" he wrote. "In the testimony which has been offered, I trust there is sufficient proof to convince every honest mind that the United States and all the great civilized nations of the world are where France was in the year 1789, and that they are rapidly 'tending' toward a revolutionary abyss even more horrible than that into which she was plunged.

"That time is known as the Reign of Terror; but the storm which is now about to break upon the world is described in Holy Writ as 'a time of trouble, such as never was.' It will be a time of strife, bloodshed, anarchy, murder, and rapine within the nations, and of universal war between the nations. Every element of trouble will be let loose."[16]

He felt that the rise of trusts and business monopolies was a prelude to the time of trouble.[17] "This decree has not yet gone forth," he wrote. "Nevertheless the period of time in which it is to go forth has even now been reached. The train has already been laid by means of which this decree can be executed in the twinkling of an eye… The great trusts and combines, of which scores have been formed during the last few months, form the train, and are a part of the machine. By them every necessity of life is

---

13 Ibid., June 24, 1890, p. 391.
14 Ibid., July 29, 1890, p. 470.
15 *The Review and Herald*, February 6, 1893, p. 156.
16 *Advent Review and Sabbath Herald*, December 29, 1896, p. 823.
17 Ibid., November 1, 1898, p. 702.

controlled… The middlemen have been degraded into mere distributors for the great concerns. These great concerns have only to say to their distributors, 'Do not buy or sell' with such and such a class, and their mandate will immediately be obeyed. And if it is not obeyed by the distributor, he will no longer be permitted to distribute."[18]

His attitude toward the prophetic gift to the church showed in an important *Review* article regarding its role in Adventist Schools. "The only place to look for an answer to this question is in the Bible and the Testimonies," he wrote. "We have been told that 'the old standard-bearers are fainting and falling,' and that young men must be educated to take their places. It is, therefore, all-important that these young men have the most thorough knowledge of the Testimonies that can possibly be given them."[19]

He felt that *Testimonies for the Church*, volume 5, could state this role much better than he. "As the end draws near, and the work of giving the last warning to the world extends, it becomes more important for those who accept present truth to have a clear understanding of the nature and influence of the Testimonies, which God, in his providence, has linked with the work of the third angel's message from its very rise."[20]

Magan himself would personify that link.

Philosophy of Education

Following the direction of the Spirit of Prophecy led to some innovations at Battle Creek College. "I have felt … that if we would pay less attention to the Latin and Greek Classics—Homer, Plato, Virgil, etc., and spend more time on the Bible, the English language, the principles of governments, vocal culture, and such lines as would be of practical benefit to us in daily life that the time and means of our students would be better expended."[21]

In another letter to Willie White a few years later, he commented, "There are very, very few histories which have been written by men whom we can call real Christians. The large majority of historians are either indifferent, or else sceptics, or else infidels. The large majority of statesmen who have written upon the principles of civil and religious liberty, such as Jefferson, Washington, Madison and others, have been men who, if they were Christians in their private lives, never made much of any profession of the same in their public life. On this account, I have found it impossible to use books altogether written by men whom I could feel clear in calling true Christians."[22]

Yet Magan and Uriah Smith used the secular *Decline and Fall of the Roman Empire* to help explain the ten kingdoms of Daniel 2. "As for Gibbon's book I do not know of more than a half dozen statements in the whole thing which anyone can take exception to. There are some statements, Sr. White, which I do not like; but they are few and far between and, on the other hand, his ideas of religious liberty, on

---

18 Ibid., June 6, 1899, p. 362.
19 Ibid., December 6, 1898, p. 785.
20 Ibid.
21 Percy Magan to Willie C. White, December 29, 1892, Ellen G. White Estate.
22 Ibid., June 21, 1895.

the equality of all religious saints in the eyes of the law; his view of the Catholic church, all of these are better in his book and more true than any I have ever found anywhere else. He is always reverend in his words concerning the gospel and Christianity and as far as this particular book is concerned, it seems to me that the objections which he brings are not to true Christianity; but to the perversion of Christianity, i.e. to the papacy."[23]

He taught a lot of early church history and felt it to be an ideal medium for explaining the great Adventist truths. "The idea is that all the truth on the Sabbath, on religious liberty, on baptism, on the state of the dead, and a number of these points can be told in the history of the early Christians," he wrote to prominent educator W. W. Prescott. He wanted to incorporate these ideas into a book. "These truths will then be read by people with less hesitation than if we were pounding away on the questions themselves, as it is now, and yet they will be imbibing the true principles all the time that they are reading."[24]

He seemed to be in complete agreement with Ellen White on the overemphasis of Adventist healing arts by John Harvey Kellogg.

"I have no doubt that the medical missionary work is a part of the work of God, and yet it seems to me it is being pushed to the detriment of other branches. It has been set before our students as the proper thing to do, and the reason given is that if they take up this line of work, they will not be persecuted."[25]

"I understand that things are going rather hard in the American Medical Missionary College," he wrote. "The faculty are quite dissatisfied with the arbitrary way in which the President deals with everything. I understand that he has not called a faculty meeting for the last two months, but settles things by his own 'free will, mere motion, and good grace.' Undoubtedly there is a just line which should be struck between anarchy on the one hand, and despotism on the other, and between liberty on the one hand, and licentiousness on the other, but I understand that the members of the faculty of the American Medical Missionary College feel that it is as much as their life is worth to express an opinion which differs in the slightest from that of the President of the school."[26]

Heading South

Magan found the year 1899 to be important in his professional and spiritual growth, in widening his horizons, and for coming into closer agreement with Ellen White. For one thing, he and Sutherland took a trip to the South early in that year to see firsthand the work of James Edson White, older brother of Willie White, in educating Mississippi Delta blacks despite the opposition of hostile whites. They intended to encourage their students to do this type of missionary work.

"Not long since I was down South and spent some time with your brother Edson on this boat," he

---

23 Ibid.
24 Percy Magan to W. W. Prescott, April 21, 1896, Ellen G. White Estate.
25 Ibid.
26 Ibid.

wrote to Willie who was living in Australia at the time. "I believe Edson is getting along very well and is improving all the time. Professor Sutherland and myself are both going down there the middle of April in order to plan for some small schools among the colored people which must be started. Edson is working very hard and I think feels somewhat discouraged that the General Conference has taken so little interest in the matter. However, he is of better courage now, I think, since he feels that the college is going to do something and is going to send some teachers down there."[27]

By the end of the 1899 summer session, Magan wrote that 100 of the 125 students attending Battle Creek College had gone out into denominational work. "This is indeed a new order of things, one for which God has been calling a long time, and one which we feel thankful to see at last realized."[28]

Money Troubles

About this time debts on Adventist schools became a big issue. Fortunately, a successful fund raising campaign helped to relieve the strain. Magan was at the center of the effort, a prelude to his later successful campaign to bring in enough money to raise the College of Medical Evangelists in California to Grade A status.

"You little know what a hard place we are in," he wrote to Willie White. "Our creditors are angry, and we have nothing with which to pay them. Since the light has come that the Review and Herald and the General Conference are not to help us, and since the General Conference people state that they are 'in the field,' we are shut off from all sources of revenue, except what we may get through private correspondence from individuals, which is very little, and from the tuition of the students. This would be amply sufficient for us to pay the current expenses of the school, were it not for the huge debt of accumulated and accumulating interest on the debt, and the heavy insurance which we have to keep up on account of it, together with the present enormous taxes for pavements, sewerage, etc., being put in by the city."[29]

Sutherland and Magan had inherited an $80,000 debt from the Prescott administration, $50,000 of it owed to the Review for the erection of buildings, plus a north addition to the main college building. They had to pay interest plus $450 a month for insurance premiums.

Prescott, A. R. Henry of the Review, and O. A. Olsen, president of the General Conference, had approved this loan even though Ellen White had said that money for the north addition should have gone to other schools, which Magan agreed with.

He felt that the money problem would take care of itself once the school followed the divine guidelines. "We have thought many times of what you have said, that the debt on the College has come on account of wrong educational principles," he wrote to Ellen White. "We have endeavored, to the best of our ability, to cut loose from these, and we believe the Lord has blessed us in doing this."[30]

---

27 Percy Magan to Willie C. White, March 31, 1899, Ellen G. White Estate.
28 *Advent Review and Sabbath Herald*, September 12, 1899, pp. 17, 18.
29 Percy Magan to Willie C. White, August 3, 1899, Ellen G. White Estate.
30 Percy Magan to Ellen G. White, August 3, 1899, Ellen G. White Estate.

To diversify, they started schools at Marshfield, Wisconsin, and Cedar Lake, Michigan. Some Michigan conference people wanted to close Battle Creek College altogether.

The Review and Herald had grown into a huge publishing house by taking on commercial printing and that made them hesitant to hire students. The school had implemented a work-study program.

"As brethren they [the Review and Herald staff] are kind to us, and show us no ill-feeling, but they simply do not look at the principles of these things as we do," wrote Magan to Ellen White. "They feel that they are doing an enormous amount of commercial work for the outside world, and that this requires the most thoroughly trained and competent hands all the time, and that it will be detrimental to their interest to take in younger and inexperienced hands to work in the different departments. As I understand it, 40 percent of their work now is for the outside world altogether, 20 percent more for the Sanitarium and the remaining 40 percent their own work.

"We find now that since practically all of our students are working for at least a part of their expenses, and since a spirit of work has come into the school, we have but little use for the old-fashioned gymnasium exercises. Our students would rather be at useful employment than at swinging clubs or dumbbells, hence we can utilize this room to good advantage."[31]

Willie White came up with an idea of donating the proceeds from a new book Ellen White was working on—*Parables of Christ*, later published as *Christ's Object Lessons*—to relieve the debt on the schools. Magan agreed with him and offered to do the same with a new book he had just written—*Perils of the Republic*—which covered current events in the light of Bible prophecies.

"I feel burdened to present the gospel of giving to our churches, to sit down with individual families and show them the blessing of this thing, and from an entirely different standpoint from the way in which they have been accustomed to see them," he wrote to Ellen White. "I know that the Lord has given me success in raising money whenever I have had a chance to do it. Elder Covert and I raised practically all the money for the industrial school in Wisconsin, and we never had to press or urge the matter."[32] His approach was to stress "perfect commandment keeping," citing Jesus Christ as the supreme example.

His long-range plan of developing localized schools fit with Ellen White's calls to downsize Battle Creek. "We are trying to keep these schools within small and moderate bounds, and in time hope that others like them will be started in other conferences and in other places in these conferences, but we do not feel like pushing the matter too hard. This has always been our plan in regard to these schools. I think it was unfortunate that they were called state schools, but we have held exactly the same principles in regard to their size and in regard to the fact that they shall draw only from the vicinity around them, and now from the whole state—in this matter, I say, we have held exactly the same principles as you lay down for us. Now as these schools start up, they will be able to accommodate many of the youth who can not be accommodated in the little church schools, and who ought not to be brought into a place like Battle Creek. This, of course, will leave only the older class

---

31   Ibid., November 24, 1899.
32   Ibid.

of students who need a comparatively brief training to fit them for the work, to come to Battle Creek. This will make our numbers here small, but with small numbers we can reduce our faculty and all the expenses generally. I think that the medical college can use the north annex of the building to good advantage, and I believe that if they are properly approached after our reorganization has been completed and our legal matters are in good safe condition, they will purchase this building from us and the land upon which it stands, for a fair price. I also believe they will purchase our South Dormitory, that is the wooden building across the road from the College grounds, for a fair price in which to keep their medical students. This would leave us with only the old original College building, the chapel addition, and the West Hall or brick dormitory. These buildings will accommodate rooms for the church school in this place. I believe it would be a great help to us, not only in a financial way, but it would enable us to bring legitimate pressure to bear upon families who want to flock in here for the privileges of the school, so that we can tell them that their children must go to the industrial schools, where they will be far better off than here. The class of students then which we would have to handle would be the older and more stable class, who would be better fitted to withstand the temptations in Battle Creek, than the ordinary run of students."[33]

Implementing this program may have pleased Ellen White, but it brought Magan and Sutherland into direct conflict with their General Conference superiors.

"However, at the last general council here the paragraph in your mother's letter to Elder Haskell, above referred to, was used as condemnatory of anything in the line of the state or industrial school. We knew that this use of the testimonies was a gross violation of them."[34]

Even though some of the General Conference leaders did not agree with Magan and Sutherland's leadership, they did approve the selling of *Christ's Object Lessons* to help relieve the debt at the schools. The vote was passed by the General Conference Committee on April 5, 1900; they also delegated a commission to oversee the project. The book itself was published on September 1, 1900.

Magan, secretary of the commission, was excited about the project. "I think the book will be a beautiful creation of its kind. The illustrations are to my mind very pleasing… Figures of Christ and the angels have been avoided as per the request of your mother, and the illustrations are natural scenes. The cover design is very fine. We are going to use a dull green cloth about the color of the back of an oak leaf. In the center of the side-cover is a beautiful mountain lily, the stem being in gold and the flowers in red. This will be enclosed in a frame of gold lines… This side cover … is emblematic of the thought which runs through the book, and which is the key-note of the title. The words cross the lily, which was one of the objects used by Christ in his lessons to the multitude. On the back of the book are golden wheat-stems and heads crossing each other."[35]

He spent the next three years hoping to motivate 70,000 church members to sell 300,000 copies of *Christ's Object Lessons*.

---

33 Ibid.
34 Ibid.
35 Percy Magan to Willie C. White, August 16, 1900, Ellen G. White Estate.

By 1900, he was spending so much time in the field pushing Christ's Object Lessons that the school replaced him with another business manager. By early 1903, Magan estimated that the campaign had brought in $237,910.75 and substantially reduced debts on schools such as Healdsburg, Union, and Walla Walla colleges, as well as Keene, South Lancaster, and Mount Vernon academies. Emmanuel Missionary College netted $22,393 from the sale of Christ's Object Lessons.[36]

Educational Reforms

Ellen White favored starting smaller intermediate schools in other states, something Magan had done. He reported about 200 simple church schools in operation. Ellen White also seemed to favor selling Battle Creek College to the sanitarium, something that was also eventually done.

Magan summed up the turn-of-the-century climate at Battle Creek in a letter to Ellen White. "The spiritual atmosphere here is anything but favorable for the training of even our best and most staunch young men and women for the work. They cannot help but see the condition of apostasy which exists to a very great extent in the church. They know the enmity which is in the minds of many against God's plans of education.

"They know the desire there is on the part of many even of the church members to have the old orders of things restored and to have infidel and pagan textbooks put back into the schools. They know of the parties and pleasures which are indulged in by the church members here.

"For a considerable time a conviction has been settling upon our minds that we have carried the educational work in Battle Creek about as far as it can be profitably carried. There are two reasons for this: one the spiritual condition of matters here; and another that we feel the importance of putting into practice the light given in regard to carrying on our school work in the country and away from these malarial influences."[37]

In this letter he revealed the seeds of an idea he and Sutherland would put into practice in Tennessee a few years later, a self-supporting school based on Spirit of Prophecy principles, which would be still part of the church but independent of denominational controls.

"Professor Sutherland and myself and a number of our teachers here feel a deep burden to take hold of this work on the self-supporting plan. We would want, of course, to have the school plant held in trust by some proper organization, and would want to carry on the work with the co-operation and under the direction of the General Conference. But we feel that God has called upon us to set an example to our brethren by working on a self-supporting basis ourselves; and we have faith, good heart and courage to do this. For the last few years, our schooling in poverty has been good discipline for us, nor has the lesson been lost. The experience we have had in this institution during this time has taught us to value money as never before.

"We also believe that if some of us who have been dependent upon the regular denominational funds for our support for so many years will set a good example in this thing it will stimulate our

---

36 *Advent Review and Sabbath Herald*, April 28, 1903.
37 Percy Magan to Ellen G. White, August 16, 1900, Ellen G. White Estate.

brethren to go to work and take hold of this self-supporting work."[38]

He, Sutherland, and fellow teacher Bessie DeGraw would do this very thing later on in Madison, Tennessee.

Yet, any suggestion of moving Battle Creek College seemed to stir up bitter opposition for a time, reminding Magan to the 1888 misunderstanding of righteousness by faith.

"The same is true now. Things which are beautiful, things which are reasonable, things which, if the common people could only be told them in their simplicity, would be received with gladness, are not discerned by many in responsible places.

"Those opposing reorganizing Battle Creek College accused reformers of "being thieves, robbers, and swindlers, and even lawsuits were started against us in the civil courts by our own brethren.

"At present our opposition comes from many of our own leading brethren, whom we love and respect, and who we believe are honest men. But Sr. White, they do not see, they do not understand."[39]

During these years Magan and Sutherland had been quietly looking for a favorable rural site to move the college, which had outgrown the cramped quarters in Battle Creek. The 1901 General Conference session approved moving the school with the full backing of Ellen White.

"Changes will have to be made," she said at the session. "But it is hard to break away from old habits and practices; and there are those who have felt inclined to stubbornly resist everything in this line. I am glad to say that Brother Magan and Brother Sutherland have made advancement in reform… I would say to Brother Magan and Brother Sutherland, You are not to think that you have made a failure in the school. Circumstances have been of a character to cause some misunderstanding."[40]

Magan announced to Willie White in June 1901 that the Battle Creek Sanitarium had agreed to take over the college property, paying $5,000 a year for its use and doing the upkeep up to $100,000.

He also closely informed Ellen White about the school relocation and sought her continual counsel. "The general opinion seems to be that we should settle somewhere in the southwestern part of Michigan or northern Indiana in the fruit belt. Excellent transportation facilities are near Benton Harbor and St. Joseph. Other considerations were distance from town, amount and price of land."[41]

By the end of June they had made the final decision on school relocation. "There seems to be a general consensus of opinions that the vicinity of Berrien Springs, Mich., would be about the best place to locate. Berrien Springs is situated in Berrien County, which is the southwestern county of the state, and is about 15 miles from the cities of St. Joseph and Benton Harbor. We can get magnificent fruit land there for $85 an acre, and we can also get some timber land, which will be very advantageous to us for fuel."[42]

Magan described the removal of the college to Berrien Springs as "an event which … marks an era in our educational work." They named the new school Emmanuel Missionary College, "a new and more

---

38 Ibid.
39 Ibid., October 24, 1900.
40 General Conference Bulletin, May 7, 1901, p. 298.
41 Percy Magan to Ellen G. White, June 1, 1901, Ellen G. White Estate.
42 Ibid., June 30, 1901.

expressive title," proclaimed the *Review*, which announced the move in July 1901.[43] "This new school must be the Avondale of America," Magan told Ellen White in a letter dated July 14, 1901.

Unfortunately, even after the move, actual cooperation from their General Conference superiors seemed hard to obtain. "Your mother urged us to start the Emmanuel Missionary College, and I know God is in the move, and I see a great future before the work," Magan wrote to Willie White. "All our leading brethren seem in harmony with it, and in fact, I know they are in harmony with the idea; but when it comes to giving us help everyone of them seems to have so many things that are, perhaps, a little nearer and dearer to them that they give all the help to these other things, and we have to shuffle for ourselves."[44]

Magan's Personal Crisis

The challenges Magan faced with his work at Emmanuel Missionary College were amplified by the personal crisis in his home with his sick wife.

"You will be very sorry to hear that my wife is desperately ill," Magan wrote to Willie White on June 15, 1903. "She has congestion of the brain, and is out of her mind all the time. She has been in this shape for two weeks. I have not said anything about it in my previous letters, hoping that she might rally quickly, and that I might be able to throw my whole strength into my work again. However, it looks now as if it was the will of God that we should have a serious time relative to her case. It will be a long time before she is strong again."

Magan was thirty-six years old at the time. Since becoming an Adventist in 1886, he had finished his education at Battle Creek College, traveled around the world evaluating Adventist missions with Haskell, taught Bible and history, written many articles and a few books, and risen to be dean of Battle Creek College in close association with his college roommate, Sutherland, who served as president. He had also traveled cross-country promoting the sale of *Christ's Object Lessons* and *Education* to help alleviate large debts on several Adventist colleges. Then, in direct obedience to the revelations of Ellen White, he had helped move Battle Creek College to Berrien Springs. All of this he had taken in stride, even when some disagreed with him, but now he faced a personal crisis that hit him hard.

"I am doing my best between my work and watching over her," he continued. "We have the best help obtainable, in the line of Sanitarium doctors and nurses, but even then the care on me is great. I have to give quite a little time to my boys, as I cannot leave them to themselves. We are praying that God will spare her, for we need her so much.

"I cannot understand why this affliction has been allowed to come, but am not questioning it at all," he concluded. "Ida was enjoying the best religious experience of her life when she was taken down. She has always been a good woman, devoted to her home, her husband, and her children, but during the last three months she has almost seemed to walk with God, and this experience is hard indeed."[45]

---

43 *Advent Review and Sabbath Herald*, July 30, 1901, p. 498.
44 Percy Magan to Ellen G. White, September 12, 1901, Ellen G. White Estate.
45 Ibid., June 15, 1903.

Unfortunately, things would get harder. "I have been made very sad by hearing from Sister Druillard of your wife's sickness," Ellen White wrote to him on June 21. Then, sensing that the excessive criticism for following her guidelines might have something to do with it, she added, "I am sincerely sorry that your wife has been so troubled by the reports that she has heard." Mrs. White hoped to alleviate the situation with the assurance of her support. "I wish to tell her and you that I am not two-sided. I have said nothing to anyone in disparagement of you or of Brother Sutherland. The fear I have had for you is that you would take too many burdens."

Someone had misinterpreted these corrective comments and told Ida Magan that Ellen White disapproved of her husband and Sutherland. That comment hurt so much that Ida lost her reason. It was in her June 21 letter to Magan that Ellen White tried to clarify things.

"I have always had the very tenderest feelings for you, my brother. I have ever regarded you as the Lord's workman, and my only fear for you now is that in your intense effort to make a success of the sale of Education, you will disqualify yourself physically for the lines of work that the school demands of you. I want you to be successful in the work of your school; or rather, in the work of the Lord's school; for in the Berrien Springs School, God desires to fit young men and young women to accomplish a precious work for Him."

Ellen White did hammer him into shape, but it was not because she was unsupportive of his work or felt that he was headed in the wrong direction. "Brother Magan, you have a family, and you should give your wife and children time and attention," she advised. "You should take time to rest. I entreat you to do this. Do not ruin your health. Stop before you reach the breaking point. Tell your wife that the Lord has a tender care for her."

She continued, "You cannot have understood the words that I spoke in the Pacific Press Chapel. They were spoken to guard you from the danger of taking too much responsibility. I desired to keep you from loading yourself down with so many burdens that the strain upon you would be greater than you could bear. What I wished to impress upon you was the thought that in your school work you are to unite and combine with other minds, that you may have sufficient workers to carry the work forward symmetrically. Every part of the work is to stand out clear and distinct, in its own individuality. One man is not to be expected to have exactly the same train of thought that another man has. One may have tact and ability that the other does not possess. The Lord will prepare workers to fit into their lot and place, for each one has his work.

"You are in danger of looking unfavorably upon some whom the Lord desires to unite with you; for fear that they will counterwork your work. Varied gifts must be brought in. You need these gifts in the work that you are doing.... It is the Lord's plan that there shall be unity in diversity. There is no man who can be a criterion for all other men."[46]

Magan's detractors had apparently taken this to mean that Sister White regarded his educational reforms as being too extreme.

---

46   Ellen G. White to Percy Magan, June 21, 1903, Ellen G. White Estate.

He and Sutherland started their manual training program at Battle Creek College, but they lost popularity by turning a playing field into a garden.[47] They tried teaching English, science, and math only from the Bible, and they even stopped granting degrees to break a papal tradition of church and state alliance.[48] Other reforms included furnishing student work opportunity by buying an 80-acre farm and starting a broom factory and tailor shop as well as dress making and printing departments.[49]

"Percy took his physical exercise and got his recreation as a student by doing useful and profitable work," Sutherland recalled years later. "He entered the college bakery and was soon chief baker. While working in the kitchen he learned to be a fair cook. He also worked in the machine shop and became efficient with many tools. My physical exercise and recreation were on the football and baseball grounds. He felt a burden to help me see that true recreation could come only when we had done something worthwhile that could be a blessing to someone. In time he succeeded in converting me and together we had the satisfaction later of operating three colleges on the work-and-study basis."[50]

Ellen White, however, clearly endorsed the work of Sutherland and Magan. Willie White wrote to him that "Mother is much interested in the progress of your industries, and she pleads that our brethren throughout the field, who are successful farmers, mechanics, and business men, shall turn their talents of money, experience, and skill to the establishment of church schools, which shall be surrounded with industries that will enable the students to earn their tuition in part or in whole."[51]

As a prominent leader Magan had received criticism like this for years, but he never thought it would adversely affect his wife. He poured out his feelings regarding the matter to the Whites, which revealed powerful spiritual growth in his life.

"Ida was taken ill quite suddenly on the night of Monday, June 1," he wrote. "The doctors pronounced the malady to be acute mania, brought on by over anxiety and worry, and lack of nutrition. At first, of course, we were terribly shocked, but as soon as I could get away alone, and seek the Lord, it was made so plain to me that He loved us, and would deal with us in great mercy. Light filled my soul, and I felt peaceful and happy. She has always been a most devoted wife and mother, and I believe, a sincerely good woman—quiet and unassuming."[52]

In looking back, he could see several preliminary events that could have contributed to her sickness, and yet, through it all, he maintained his religious equilibrium.

Ida had nursed Magan through a long bout of typhoid fever during the autumn of 1901. Also,

---

47   Emmett K. Vande Vere, *The Wisdom Seekers* (Nashville, TN: Southern Publishing Association, 1972), p. 83.

48   Ibid., p. 85.

49   Chronological arrangement of events in the life of Percy Tilson Magan and those associated with him, as told by Edward A. Sutherland, Center for Adventist Research, Andrews University, Berrien Springs, Michigan.

50   Edward A. Sutherland, M.D., "My Sixty Years' Friendship with Percy T. Magan," *The Journal, Alumni Association College of Medical Evangelists*, March 1948.

51   *Advent Review and Sabbath Herald*, January 23, 1900, p. 60.

52   Percy Magan to Ellen G. White, July 1, 1903, Ellen G. White Estate.

"the death of her brother, about a year ago, just after he had graduated as a physician, was a great shock to her. This, together with my long sickness, and the recent reports which were circulated about me, I think, did the work."[53]

A glimmer of hope appeared after approximately a month of her becoming ill. "Thank God, she is now better," Magan continued. "Her mind has returned, and although she is very, very weak, and terribly shattered, yet with care we know that God will give her back to us again. It will be a long time before she is able to keep house, and if I can get money enough together, I will send her to California this autumn, if she is strong enough to go at that time."[54]

Magan had no intention of blaming his problems on his detractors, but their words had clearly had an effect. "I had not written you a word about the reports which were being circulated because I felt that if we would take them in the right spirit, they would only do us good anyway, and that time would reveal that they [the reports] were false. No, I never thought, for one moment, that you were two-sided, untrue or false. I did, of course, think that possibly God had revealed to you things relative to me that you had not had opportunity to tell me, but I know that you were never the author of these reports the way they were circulated; but they came from such high quarters, and have been told so widely, with such assurance that we felt it was absolutely no use to endeavor to counteract them, and therefore decided to simply pray to God for grace, and wait until in His own good time He should clear the clouds away.

> He and Sutherland knew they had done right by getting out of Battle Creek, which he described as "a seething, foaming mass of lying reports, unbelief, backbiting, criticism, and disregard for the plain commands of God."

"Even if you had spoken disparagingly of Brother Sutherland and myself, we would not think anything strange of that, for the reason that we know that our work has been very imperfect, and very faulty."[55]

He and Sutherland knew they had done right by getting out of Battle Creek, which he described as "a seething, foaming mass of lying reports, unbelief, backbiting, criticism, and disregard for the plain commands of God."[56]

He seemed to have the same opinion of some Adventists there as they had of him. "I tremble for the institutions which are there, and we are constantly offering prayers to God that He will spare Dr. Kellogg and the Sanitarium, and turn the great mistake of rebuilding that institution in Battle Creek,

---

53   Ibid.
54   Ibid.
55   Ibid.
56   Ibid.

even yet, into a precious victory."[57]

By following Ellen White every step of the way, he and Sutherland had been brought under close scrutiny by church leaders, and this left them no margin for error. "We are being watched on every side, and we know that a number of our leading brethren will give us no rest if we go in debt at all, and we are straining every nerve to keep out of debt."[58]

But things once again went sour even before he could complete his long letter to Ellen White. "(Since writing the above my poor wife has been taken much worse again. We are going to have a season of prayer for her recovery.)"[59]

Just a few weeks later, Magan wrote again to Ellen White. "I do not know what to do with my poor children. They are very good and make us no trouble, and the girl I have keeping house for me does real well. She is a good Christian girl, and a fairly good housekeeper, but with four and five nurses in the house all the time it keeps her so busy cooking and doing the housework that there is but little time left for either her or I to teach the children and this I feel must not be neglected. Dr. Kellogg declares that Ida will come out all right, but says that it may be some time. She seems to be wearing out very fast. We know that you are praying for her, and feel so thankful."[60]

"My poor wife continues just about the same," Magan shared with Ellen White as the summer progressed. "She is still out of her mind and suffers terribly in her mind, although we do not think she suffers very much physically, but, of course, we cannot tell. Sometimes she is quite violent, so much so that it takes three or four persons to control and care for her. Her strength is keeping up fairly well, but she looks haggard and worn, and of course the strain is terrible on the rest of us. Poor girl, it breaks my heart to see her thus. We are praying earnestly for her, and believe that God in His own good time and way will send relief."[61]

Yet even at this point, he refused to let this experience embitter him. "I hope you will not think that I have any hard feelings toward any one on account of her sickness, or on account of the causes which have brought it on, for I have not.

"I believe that God's hand is over us for good, and that He doth not willingly afflict the children of men, and that those whom he loveth he chasteneth and scourgeth every son whom he receiveth."[62]

Although his faith held firm, it was clearly a struggle, and he questioned if he was doing anything wrong when he was following the guidance of the Spirit of Prophecy.

"We are following your advice strictly relative to the care of my dear one. I have only Christian nurses caring for her. We have four of them—two in the day and two in the night. They are good women, all of them God-fearing Christian nurses, and they do everything they can for her. We are using the

---

57   Ibid.
58   Ibid.
59   Ibid.
60   Ibid., July 20, 1903.
61   Ibid., August 2, 1903.
62   Ibid.

hygienic treatments altogether. We keep her in neutral baths when we can; we give her neutral sheet packs at other times, and keep ice on her head and throat when necessary; and keep her feet and hands warm with hot bags when the circulation is poor. She has plenty of sunshine and air, and in her quiet moments the nurses take her out a little bit in the yard for a walk.

"At times she is very violent. The poor girl seems to feel that a power is trying to take her life, and this makes us feel all the more that it is the work of Satan. At times she feels she must escape from this power by jumping from the window, getting away from the house, or putting an end to her own life. If we would let her, she would have choked herself many times. Then again she is quiet and calm, and we read the Bible to her, and she repeats chapter after chapter after us, and smiles as she listens to the promises of God. Often, even in the midst of her mania, she asks us to pray for her, and she will watch us with the saddest, sweetest smile while we are praying. It is wonderful the way she remembers scripture, and the way she will repeat it. I know that God will hear our prayers, and that He will heal and help; her, and we will never rest pressing our petitions to his throne.

"Her strength keeps up fairly well, but she has bruised and torn her body terribly when these awful spells have been upon her. The doctors say there are many cases just like hers, and that they come from grief and anxiety.

"Yes, I am keeping cheerful and happy, although at times the trial is a sore one. It fills me with sadness to see her looking so worn and torn and haggard, her body bruised and cut, for we cannot prevent this when these terrible struggles come. But I am resting in the Lord, for I know He hears our prayers, and that He doeth all things well."[63]

Sadly, healing didn't come. "I long to understand better how to grasp his promises," he continued in the agony of this trying experience similar to what had afflicted Job. "I long to know what faith means better than I do. It seems to me so many times that if I were where I should be, God could rebuke in a moment of time these awful powers of darkness, and save my poor darling from all this suffering. The kind words in your letter, that God was not displeased with us, have cheered me greatly in many a dark hour. I have been tempted at times to think all this has come about on account of our sins; and yet God knows we have tried to walk aright before him."[64]

Ida continued to deteriorate, and Magan felt obliged to take their two boys to live with her parents in California. His spiritual journey continued through this trying time.

"It was Friday, Oct. 9, when you bid me good bye at the station at St. Helena," he wrote to Ellen White. "I felt very sad and very lonely as I left you. It seemed when I left my poor little children at Santa Ana that the last thing I had on earth was being taken from me, and coming back here to my home at Berrien Springs seemed almost like coming to the grave; but in the midst of it all the thought came over me so often of how good God was, and how tenderly he had always dealt with us and that I must learn to know Him now, and to trust Him more than I had ever done before. I knew that these trials are sent to us not to bring bitterness out of our characters, but to bring all the fragrance that God can possibly

---

63   Ibid., August 17, 1903.
64   Ibid.

bring into our lives, and I want the sorrows through which I am passing now to have this effect upon me."[65]

Ida continued going downhill, and, upon the advice of his physicians, Magan moved her into a mental hospital in Kalamazoo, Michigan. This turned out to be another step forward spiritually. "I feel very lonely and sad and very broken in spirit," he commented. "I am settling down here, however, to hard work. The Lord has blessed me with a deep Christian experience during the last few weeks, and I feel an intense desire to labor spiritually for our students and members of our faculty."[66]

Home troubles led Magan to decline reappointment as secretary to the Relief of Schools Committee later on that year, a position requiring much promotional travel to encourage the sale of Ellen White's books. Ida was getting worse, and he wanted to devote his time to the Berrien Springs school, and he did not want to be too far from his wife.[67]

"It is true that my home is now broken up, but I can dispose of these I am sure to good advantage. Bro. and Sister Hill (the brother who has charge of the mechanical work in our printing office) are now living in my house. They have the downstairs and I am boarding with them. They are splendid people and are very kind to me, indeed, and do everything in their power to make the place just as homelike as possible. I have all the upstairs rooms rented except the study and the little north bedroom, which I use for my own sleeping apartment. This takes some load off me as far as finances are concerned. I do not expect that I will make any money off the house, but will have plenty to cover all the affixed charges, keep up repairs and depreciation, and I feel that I am, indeed, blessed to have things in this shape.

"Sometimes it seems very hard to bear up under all of this affliction. From a human standpoint I cannot understand it, but God knows what is best. I am thankful, however, that God is giving me a blessed experience out of it all. He has seemed so much nearer and dearer to me the last two weeks than before for many years."[68]

As 1903 came to a close and 1904 began, Ida's condition dramatically deteriorated. "I am in deep trial over my wife," Magan wrote to Ellen White. "About a week ago I received a letter from the doctor at the hospital stating that she had taken a turn for the worse, and that she seemed to have developed tuberculosis. They have found a considerable quantity of tubercular baccilli in her sputum, and she has already lost over 10 pounds. She has a fever from 102 to 103 every afternoon and evening. We greatly fear that the poor child will not last long. Her mind is in such a condition that it is impossible to move her either to Colorado or California. It all seems so inexpressibly sad that I cannot bear to write about it, so will say no more for the present. God has been very good to me in this affliction and is sustaining me. He knows just what is best, and I can only go on clinging to Him and wait the carrying out of His will."[69]

By the end of April, Ida clearly had little time left, but Magan still presented a clear picture of

---

65   Ibid., October 29, 1903.
66   Percy Magan to Willie C. White, November 11, 1903, Ellen G. White Estate.
67   Percy Magan to A. G. Daniells and Willie C. White, November 24, 1903.
68   Percy Magan to Willie C. White and Ellen G. White, November 30, 1903, Ellen G. White Estate.
69   Percy Magan to Ellen G. White, April 13, 1904, Ellen G. White Estate.

someone resting fully on Christ.

"We have always been passionately devoted to each other and our married life has been a most happy one, but God knows what is best and I can only say with one of old, 'The Lord gave and the Lord hath taken, blessed be the name of the Lord.'

"When I think of some of the things which have helped to cause her loss, which need never have been (the wretched stories that I had given up the truth and that you had gone back of Prof. Sutherland and I and that her sickness was a judgment of God on account of our wickedness) it seems hard to be reconciled, but I have said nothing about these things, as it does no good."[70]

The Formation of Madison

Ida Magan died on May 19, 1904, during a high-level church meeting at Berrien Springs. Elder A. T. Jones conducted her funeral service on a Sabbath afternoon. The next day, during a morning service, Magan, to the disappointment of Ellen White, followed his friend Sutherland in publicly resigning their positions at Emmanuel Missionary College to go off on their own and start a school somewhere in the South.

Ellen White chided them for maintaining a hostile attitude toward the top church leaders like A. G. Daniells and Prescott, but she supported their move to the South and helped them find a location for their new enterprise about twelve miles outside of Nashville, Tennessee. She then wrote an article for the Review showing her support.

"Let us sustain Brethren Sutherland and Magan in their efforts to advance this important work," she advised. "As these brethren go to the South to take hold of pioneer work in a difficult field, we ask our people to make their work as effective as possible by assisting them in the establishment of a school near Nashville."[71]

Magan and Sutherland continued implementing their educational reforms in the underprivileged South with only a token of an Adventist presence. But through it all they closely consulted with Ellen White, as always. A *Review* article summed up their work as "to put up their own buildings, cultivate the land, go out and canvass for books, and thus pay their way; to take in those of more or less experience as assistants, to go through the preliminary work of education, and become self-supporting laborers to go out in various localities in the South, where poor educational facilities exist, procure land, start schools, invite in pupils, teach these how to raise crops, fruit, etc., and do work on intelligent plans."[72]

Criticism and opposition continued, but Ellen White did all she could to encourage them and keep their critics at bay.

Money was scarce, and life at Madison meant hard work outdoors as well as in. Giving up conference subsidies meant going to other places for money or earning it themselves on the farm. Sutherland wrote years later that at the beginning, Magan had charge of the farm, Sutherland the dairy, and

---

70 Ibid., April 29, 1904.
71 *Advent Review and Sabbath Herald,* August 18, 1904, p. 8.
72 Ibid., March 30, 1905, p. 18.

DeGraw the poultry.

Magan again showed how he could maintain a good attitude amid difficult circumstances.

"Besides, when a man gets up at four thirty in the morning, and works in the field with a team of mules till one o'clock, and then goes at it again till six-thirty p.m., and then conducts a study for an hour or an hour and a half; takes the responsibility of planning the work for the boys, he is doing a pretty good days work," he wrote to Willie White. "And when it is taken into account that this has had to be done on old, and rather worn out land, with a goodly sprinkle of rocks and thorn bushes, and by one who has not followed the farming business since he was 18 years of age, I, at least, find that it has taxed my determination of purpose, and capacity to meet and overcome hard problems even more than heading a relief of schools campaign. And this becomes all the sterner when you haven't a penny of money, and have been asked not to push your claims for the same till a Hundred Thousand Dollar Fund has been made up. I have realized that some apparently small things may test a man's endurance and power to bring about results, and carry through an undertaking much more than some seemingly large ones. But the whole has been a great experience, and I feel more genuine iron determination, and grim strenuously in my bones today to take hold of things which need to be done and to do them."[73]

Getting Into Medicine

In the fall of 1905 Magan married Lillian Eshleman, a staff physician at the Battle Creek Sanitarium who became instrumental in carrying out another Ellen White directive soon after they had purchased their property in the South.

"We greatly desire the prosperity of the work in the South," Ellen White wrote to them. "You have our prayers and our influence to help you begin your work near Nashville. It may be that a sanitarium might be erected on the land you have purchased, for it is not too far from Nashville. Thus the land could be more fully utilized, and the work of the two institutions might blend together."[74]

Sutherland had wanted to do that in Berrien Springs after fire destroyed the Battle Creek Sanitarium. Ellen White had mentioned starting over in a smaller setting, but that turned out to be too radical a reform for the church in Michigan. Now that he and Magan were on their own, they could do this.

They obviously needed doctors, and Dr. Lillian Magan helped make it possible for them to start a sanitarium on the campus in 1909, the first patient being a local man wanting Battle Creek-type treatments. Another physician and college friend, Dr. Newton Evans, moved onto campus and established a medical practice there as well as taught pathology at the University of Tennessee medical school in Nashville.

This need for physicians turned their attention to Loma Linda, which Ellen White had been instrumental in founding a year after she helped them get going at Madison. Loma Linda's medical school was struggling and needed Evans on its staff, but he didn't want to leave Madison in a lurch. He felt that

---

73 Percy Magan to Willie C. White, September 7, 1905.
74 Ellen G. White to Percy Magan and E. A. Sutherland, August 6, 1904, Ellen G. White Estate.

Sutherland and Magan, especially Magan, ought to fill the physician gap by taking the medical course, and he agreed to remain at Madison long enough for them to finish their training.

Ellen White agreed. "She advised them to go ahead and take it in one of the colleges in Nashville saying that they were men of experience and well founded in the faith and that they would come in contact with men who in later years would be valuable friends," Sutherland wrote in an autobiographical sketch.[75]

This prediction literally came true just a few short years later after Magan became dean of the Los Angeles campus of the College of Medical Evangelists.

"I have always had a kind of horror of a man who has been engaged in the ministry for years taking up the Medical work or any other line of work as he may have less interest in the ministerial work and not amount to very much in the medical work," he wrote once again to Willie White after thinking it over. "We feel, however, that God has a special mission for us in the medical work. I do not intend to give up the ministry. I intend to continue my study and research. But as you say the time has come for great medical evangelical movement and I do not see how this is going to be unless some of those who have had experience in the evangelical work take up the medical work. Our young men who take up the medical work have never had the experience necessary to make them powerful in uniting the medical and the evangelical."[76]

The plan called for four years at the University of Tennessee medical school in Nashville and later in Memphis during their senior year. Evans taught there and other faculty members knew about them through the sanitarium. They had pre-med credits and rode motorcycles to school every day. Nellie Druillard, Bessie DeGraw, and William Rocke handled details on the Madison campus while Magan and Sutherland were studying.

In the meantime Magan kept up his ministerial work by writing a series of articles on the "Eastern Question." The *Watchman Magazine*, published in Nashville, offered a complete set to its readers. Titles included "Russia's Struggle for the Sea," "The Question of the Far East," and "The Kings from the Rising of the Sun," as well as "The Policy of Japan."

These articles continued after he started medical school in 1910, and he, along with many other Adventist evangelists, proclaimed the Turkish Ottoman Empire as the "The King of the North" in Daniel 11. He marveled that the Ottomans had built up an empire twice the size of Europe minus Russia, which included Egypt and Libya, as mentioned in this Old Testament prophecy. He felt that the fall of the Ottoman Empire meant the end of the world.

"The mighty Word of God had said that the passing of Turkey would mark the advent of a time of trouble such as never was since there was a nation even to that same time," he commented in a 1911

---

75 Chronological arrangement of events in the life of Percy Tilson Magan and those associated with him, as told by Edward A. Sutherland, Center for Adventist Research, Andrews University, Berrien Springs, Michigan.

76 Percy Magan to Willie C. White, September 23, 1910, Ellen G. White Estate.

Review article explaining why Russia had lost the Crimean War during the nineteenth century.[77] It was not yet time for Turkey to fall.

The *Review* and Ellen White seemed satisfied with the Madison work. "They [Sutherland and Magan] have a good location for their school and sanitarium, where there are over seventy students in training for the hill-country schools. Already a number of schools have been started for the poor whites in the hills, in each of which there are from twenty to sixty students in attendance. The sanitarium, though small, answers their purpose well, and is filled with patients. The work on the farm, in the school, and in the sanitarium, is done entirely by student help. This affords all an education of a practical nature,—just such an education as they need to work successfully for the poor people in the hills."[78]

Ellen White wrote the following to Magan, "I pray that the Lord's blessing may rest upon you. Your work has been made disagreeable and difficult because of the attitude of some of your brethren. The Lord has not prompted these things that are of a discouraging nature. I have written to you in harmony with the Light that I have received for years, but I ask you not to use this in a way that might be injudicious. I feel assured that you will act with proper discretion in this matter."[79]

In this same letter she hinted at the role ahead of him in the Adventist medical work. "The Lord is not pleased with a division between medical missionary physicians and gospel workers. By some, strange walls have been built up. We should study to reach the unity of the faith. Truth will bear away the victory on every point."[80]

The Medical Work

His medical school experience underlined in his mind the counsels of Ellen White on the dangers of sending Adventist young people to state medical schools. He described them as "bad places, although there are many good people connected with them. There is much smoking, chewing, swearing, course and obscene language. Nevertheless the work has opened up to me truths which I have read in the Bible and testimonies for years in a way that is little short of marvelous."[81]

As always, Magan took his share of criticism for going into medicine. Some of his friends and followers in places like the Northern Union, where he had visited many camp meetings, wondered if he wanted something more lucrative than teaching. He hoped that Ellen White could perhaps help him with this problem. To head off some criticism, Sutherland and Magan chose the inconvenience of riding to school on motorcycles instead of buying a car.

"We have not taken up this work because we wanted something easier, or because we are tired of the work we are now doing, but only that we might be able to do that work better," he wrote to Willie

---

77 *The Advent Review and Sabbath Herald*, March 23, 1911, p. 6.
78 Ibid., March 9, 1911, p. 18.
79 Ellen G. White to Percy Magan, May 15, 1907, Ellen G. White Estate.
80 Ibid.
81 Percy Magan to Willie C. White, October 3, 1910, Ellen G. White Estate.

White.[82]

Magan turned down some good job offers after completing his training, including a position at a new medical school the University of the South wanted to start in Nashville. "I have refused it, as I have only one thing in my head and that is to do what I can the remaining years of my life to eternally push the work among these poor people in the hills," he wrote to Willie White on October 3, 1910.

A few years later, Magan wrote, "We are all very much interested in the work at Loma Linda. We have watched its rise and progress with a keen joy." Then showing that two years in a state school had not dimmed his Adventist vision, he added, "I certainly hope that the medical course will not swallow up the old medical evangelistic course. This is one thing they will need to guard against."[83]

He had another reason to take a serious interest in Loma Linda. "I am planning, if we can get together enough money, to send my eldest boy, Wellesley, there next year. I would not have him in one of these worldly medical schools for the world. I don't know of anything more wicked on the face of the earth than the ordinary worldly medical school."[84]

The next year Loma Linda accepted his son, which placed him under a financial strain, for he and Wellesley were both attending medical school during the 1913-14 school year, but as with other challenges in life, Magan did not complain.

Earning his medical degree in 1914 brought Magan into the midst of the struggling, developing situation at the new medical school in Loma Linda. Here he would test his faith in Ellen White at its highest levels.

His friend Willie White was closely involved with Loma Linda. The board had started the first two years of instruction at Loma Linda, but the school needed a teaching hospital in a more populated area. That pointed toward Los Angeles, and Willie White seemed to feel that Magan should take charge there.

Magan himself was not so sure. "In the first place I have but little confidence in myself as an organizer and leader," he wrote to Willie White in discouraging the idea. "The tremendous needs of this kind of work and the problems to be grappled with appall me as I think of them. I am not much of a reformer. If I am certain that the Spirit of Prophecy points in a certain direction, I ask God for grace to lead me and give me strength to follow in the light... "[85]

Such a position would require a good working relationship with the General Conference officers, something Magan had never had.

"There was a day as you know when I was prominently connected with large enterprises in the General Conference, but my experience with the General Conference brethren has been anything but a satisfactory one," he continued. "I find myself shrinking as I think of going into lines of work where I am to be closely associated with men who have fought me at every turn of the road for 10 long years. If

---

82　Ibid.
83　Ibid., June 20, 1912.
84　Ibid.
85　Ibid., September 13, 1914.

these men really feel toward me as their speeches and letters indicate, I can not see how they could conscientiously agree to have me connected with their work. I cannot change my principles in regard to the work at Madison. I believe that it was born of God, and that it has been sustained by God all these years.

"I do not believe that these men who have accused me of high crimes and misdemeanors for the past 10 years will ever agree to this plan.

"I have no question but what Elder Andross and those associated with him are sincere. I am sure that there are a number of men at Washington who are at the head of the general work whose feelings toward me are such that they could not conscientiously admit me into their work.

"Again, if I were to be connected with Loma Linda I fear I should want to inaugurate some radical changes. And I cannot tell whether these would meet the minds of my brethren or not. I firmly believe that a SDA medical college ought to get into the Association of American Medical Colleges, but it can never get a better rating by the way its matters have been handled in the past."

He continued, "I thoroughly believe with you in regard to the situation among our students at Los Angeles. They need an 'inspirator' more than an 'educator.' They need to be welded to this message, to remember that they are sheep among wolves, to be carefully inspired in the right way so that they will not become enthusiastic over worldly men and their teachings."[86]

The past four years had taught him that achieving these spiritual goals would be crucial for a church-operated medical school to meet the American Medical Association (AMA) requirements.

"My medical experience is small and amounts to but little, but I have the acquaintance of a number of the leading men in the American Medical Association, and these men have a great respect for us," he wrote to Willie White. "Dr. John A. Witherspoon, who a year ago was president of the American Medical Association, calls on our sanitarium whenever he wants a nurse for his wife. Dr. Dixon, his partner, comes out to see me in consultation very often. These men I am sure can be reached.

"But they will not be reached by an attempt to copy worldly models and standards, but rather because they respect us for the kind of work which we are endeavoring to do, and because of our missionary spirit and enterprise."[87]

> "But they will not be reached by an attempt to copy worldly models and standards, but rather because they respect us for the kind of work which we are endeavoring to do, and because of our missionary spirit and enterprise."

This last statement showed the difference in attitude to Ellen White between himself and Kellogg.

Since Magan had studied under and made friends with prominent physicians like Witherspoon and William Haggard, both of whom served as presidents of the American Medical Association, and

---

86   Ibid.
87   Ibid.

Dr. Olin West, a longtime executive secretary of the AMA, the board of the Loma Linda medical school chose him to state their case to the medical profession.

Early in 1915, while Ellen White lay dying in her Elmshaven, California, home, Magan attended the Council on Medical Education, Federation of State Medical Examining Boards, and Association of American Medical Colleges in Chicago, and he described Witherspoon as being "friendly to Adventists and Loma Linda and says to 'rest easy' regard to school rating."[88]

In spite of Witherspoon's words of encouragement, an evaluating committee from the American Medical Association disapproved of the church executive officer of the board serving as school business manager, giving him administrative authority over the president and the dean, among other things. Daniells seemed to balk at making changes, even though Magan claimed that not adhering to the AMA's request could force a closing by lowering the school's rating to Grade C.

Magan later wrote about some General Conference men trying to limit attendance at the College of Medical Evangelists. "I don't suppose these men intend to be mean, but they are doing everything in their power to shut down on us," he commented. "They complained about how much money it cost to run the school and would not give any money for buildings. In a way it gets to be tiresome—trying to run an institution for men who at heart don't want it."[89]

Magan found no real conflicts between the AMA standards and the counsel of Ellen White. One such basic requirement was to have Adventist medical students study under Adventist instructors to keep the worldly influence out in a hospital owned and controlled by the school. This met with AMA requirements that students be instructed by faculty from one school, not two separate schools of medicine.

Other problems resulted in the classes taught. The AMA felt that the courses were not arranged in proper scientific manner, the anatomy laboratory was poorly located, a pathological laboratory was in need of a complete overhaul, the pharmacology course was inadequate, they operated a badly deficient library, and they had improper staff and assistants for the various departments.

The medical school's C rating meant trouble for the graduates. "I then asked Dr. Colwell what chance our students were going to have to take State Board Examinations. His reply, 'At present there are 30 states which refuse to examine students from C grade medical colleges and we intend to inaugurate a campaign immediately to get all states to refuse to examine students from the C grade schools.'

"Dr. Colwell then stated that for the present there would be only three grades of medical colleges: 'A' Acceptable medical colleges. 'B' Doubtful medical colleges. 'C' Medical colleges which are not acceptable. The 'A' grade colleges are recommended to all State Boards and are asked to admit their students to be examined. The students of the 'B' grade college are not recommended and no advice is given one way or the other concerning his chance for standing examination for State License. The states are warned and asked not to accept for examination the students from C grade schools such as Loma

---

88 Ibid., February 13, 1915.
89 Percy Magan to Lida Scott, August 4, 1921, Percy T. Magan Collection, Center for Adventist Research, Andrews University, Berrien Springs, Michigan.

Linda at that point.

"I do not see that there is any way under heaven unless God works a miracle whereby we can get out of this state of affairs," he continued to Willie White. "It does not seem to me, however, that this should cause us to lose interest or be discouraged. I kept telling Dr. Evans that no matter how hard things are that God would work something out of the whole experience."[90]

Here Magan faced the supreme challenge to his faith in Ellen White and the Spirit of Prophecy and the directives to start the medical college. But, as before, he waited for a miracle and did not allow hard times to affect his attitude.

"I have felt for a long time … that Loma Linda needs a deeper experience in the real missionary spirit of sacrifice and in God's ways of healing the sick. To my mind it would be one of the worst things in the world if Loma Linda should be able to get into the legal grade A and at the same time not be in the spiritual A grade. The heads of our graduates would be turned and they would be of little use or value to the cause of God. Consequently I cannot help but feel that this entire situation is a great blessing in a cloud of disguise. I do not suppose it is possible for our brethren at Loma Linda to prevail upon the General Conference people to spend for equipment and running expenses a sum anything like is required by the Council on Medical Education and frankly, I do not blame them for not wanting to do so. I know the argument which many of them put up, namely that the returns for the enormous amount of money necessary to be expended are altogether too small to justify such expenditures and I cannot help but feel that they make a strong argument.

> "… the teachings of the Bible clearly prove that God never asked his people to do anything impossible… but God has always fulfilled his word whenever his people have trusted him."

"I do not believe that because of the present situation, we ought to give up the idea of training men and women to meet the legal standard," he concluded. "I think we ought to go ahead and perfect our plans and our school to the very best of our ability, and give a training as far as we possibly can that will meet their requirements."[91]

That statement put him squarely in line with what Ellen White had predicted concerning Loma Linda and made him a natural choice to head up the development of the Los Angeles campus. His powerful appeal persuaded the 1915 Fall Council meeting at Loma Linda to approve accrediting the medical school, and that clinched the decision to put him in charge of the Los Angeles campus.

"The light given me is we must provide that which is essential to qualify our youth who desire to be physicians, so that they may intelligently fit themselves to be able to stand the examinations required to prove their efficiency as physicians," Ellen White had written in 1910 in response to a request for

---

90 Percy Magan to Willie C. White, March 3, 1915.
91 Ibid.

guidance on what to do about the Loma Linda medical course. "The medical school at Loma Linda is to be of the highest order … for the special preparation of those of our youth who have clear convictions of their duty to obtain a medical education that will enable them to pass the examinations required by law of all who practise as regularly qualified physicians, we are to supply whatever may be required, so that these youth need not be compelled to go to medical schools conducted by men not of our faith. Thus we shall close a door that the enemy would be pleased to have left open; and our young men and young women, whose spiritual interests the Lord desires us to safeguard, will not feel compelled to connect with unbelievers in order to obtain a thorough training along medical lines."[92]

Magan gave these words as much serious consideration as he did the American Medical Association guidelines. The way he saw it, the AMA wanted the college to do what Ellen White had said they should have been doing all along. To him, this high stakes venture was another sign of the second coming.

"In the writings given this denomination through the Spirit of Prophecy the great movements are outlined that must be made in connection with the cause of God during the closing days of earth's history," Magan wrote in the Review in announcing his plans for Loma Linda. "Many times the undertakings which were called for by the servant of the Lord have appeared to human sight so great and costly that men and women have staggered because of unbelief, and have felt that these could not be accomplished by a people so poor financially and so small numerically as ourselves.

"But the teachings of the Bible clearly prove that God never asked his people to do anything impossible of successful fulfilment," he continued. "Many times, to be sure, it has appeared upon the surface as if God's plans and purposes could not be carried out, but God has always fulfilled his word whenever his people have trusted him."[93]

Building a Grade A medical school did indeed seem impossible, but Magan's years of service through challenges and trials had transformed him into a man of powerful faith.

And trust God Magan did. While Loma Linda struggled and Battle Creek enjoyed world fame, Magan had to trust the Spirit of Prophecy and wait upon the Lord for vindication.

"It was the Lord's purpose that the Loma Linda Sanitarium should become the property of our people, and he brought it about at a time when the rivers of difficulty were full and overflowing their banks," Magan quoted from the Spirit of Prophecy. "The very fact that our leaders in the great mission fields of the Orient care calling as never before for consecrated medical missionaries is sufficient reason why we should furnish the necessary equipment for the training of these laborers. God has blessed us with many schools and colleges. These have proved a refuge and a haven for our youth, and hundreds upon hundreds within their walls have dedicated their lives to the service of God. But we have only one medical missionary training school, the one at Loma Linda. And as medical missionary work is to be the last work of mercy done by our people in the world, it is fitting that this school should be placed upon a sure and substantial footing. In this the Lord is calling upon us to 'strengthen the hands of the

---

92   *The Advent Review and Sabbath Herald*, March 17, 1910, p. 19.
93   Ibid., March 2, 1916, p. 16.

builders.'"[94]

That meant putting his faith to work by coming up with $60,000 to build the needed teaching hospital in Los Angeles. The 1915 Fall Council approved the undertaking, but did not appropriate any money toward the project. Adventist women led by Mrs. S. N. Haskell pledged themselves to raise the money for it, and they spent 1916 implementing a well-publicized fund-raising campaign, but they came up short. While Ellen White had said the church was to operate a fully accredited medical school, the Lord did not tell her where the money was coming from. She had also told the brethren not to embarrass the church with debts, to take the third angel's message to all countries overseas, and to scatter Adventist literature like the leaves of autumn.

These circumstances had put Ellen White into deep perplexity about Loma Linda. Just a few months before she died, Lida Funk Scott visited Elmshaven and made her feel better by giving $2,000 to the Loma Linda Sanitarium. The Lord did not reveal to Ellen White that Scott would give much more to the Los Angeles campus and make it a reality.

Scott was the heiress to a million-dollar estate as the daughter of Isaac Funk, co-founder of Funk & Wagnalls Publishing Co. She had become an Adventist at Battle Creek through the influence of Kellogg and had attached herself to the work of Madison about the time Sutherland and Magan finished medical school.

Sutherland, like Magan, was also a man of great faith and he was willing to put it all on the line by building a medical school many fellow believers thought humanly impossible. His part in the drama was to tell Scott that if she wanted to support Madison she must support Loma Linda. His school and sanitarium needed doctors.

Scott became one of Magan's biggest donors. While his old General Conference detractors dragged their feet on funding and complained of the enormous expenses, she sent him thousands of dollars: $3,000 for a girls dormitory named Montclair Cottage, $6,000 for a service building, $8,000 for a dietetic unit, $5,000 for a physiotherapy building and much more.[95]

After not enough money came in through the women's fund-raising effort to start hospital construction in 1916, and the United States entered World War I in 1917 with draft issues threatening to eliminate all students, the need for the teaching hospital remained the chief obstacle to getting out of that tenuous B rating.

Magan needed $60,000, and the General Conference, at its 1917 Fall Council, finally agreed to give him half that amount if he could somehow come up with the first half ($5,000 was equivalent to $100,000 today). In this hour of great need, Magan risked a twenty-eight-year close relationship with Sutherland and asked his friend if he would allow a $30,000 pledge from Scott to Madison to go to the College of Medical Evangelists.

"This was a hard request for me to agree to," Sutherland later recalled. "I recognized that it was

---

94   Ibid., p. 17.
95   Percy Magan to Lida Funk Scott, June 2, 1926, Adventist Heritage Research Center, Andrews University, Berrien Springs, Michigan.

only natural for Dr. Magan to seek help from his old Madison friends, and past experience had given us so much confidence in the integrity of each other we were bound to cooperate when one of us needed help. I was convinced that his request was reasonable, and we both went to Mrs. Scott and told her of the great need of help for the College of Medical Evangelists. She hesitated at first but soon saw that the self-supporting work in the South could not prosper without doctors and that there was no way of securing them except from the College of Medical Evangelists and so gave him $30,000."[96]

Sutherland added that "Dr. Magan saw that we got back a greater blessing than we had given to the medical school, because he personally shepherded our Madison students so well that many of them returned to the South prepared to carry on the much-needed medical missionary work."[97]

That brought in a strong middle class and helped develop the then underprivileged Southern Union into the strongest union in the North American Division, both in membership and financial strength.

Even though Magan was working at Loma Linda, he kept close ties with Madison. "Madison has been established for about 15 years now and has always had the following out of God's testimonies, both educationally and medically, for the very inspired breath of its life," he wrote to Scott in 1919. "Everything we have tried to do there, as far as God gave us light, was based upon Sister White's writings and our teachers and students there have come to realize that these writings must be the guiding star, the text, the lodestone of their every thought and act.

"When I came here I found everything different. I have not any sympathy upon the part of our leading brethren for a strong work in building up this place on the basis of the Spirit of Prophecy. The first fight was to get something started at all in order to insure to our people a denominational medical school. You know well the struggle we had at the General Conference Council in Loma Linda in 1915 when the Hospital was born, and I am sure you will remember my letters to you relative to the struggle again at the General Conference council in the fall of 1916 in Washington when the brethren voted not to build the Hospital, even although a year before they had voted to build it, and when they voted only to give two years of medical work and to let the students go to worldly schools for the rest of their educating. The next struggle I had in my hands was to get buildings for this place. First of all only half a block of land was bought and I was forbidden to purchase any more and was told that all the money must be saved for one large concrete building before anything could be done. Had I let myself be throttled in this manner there would have been no College of Medical Evangelists today. God knows the truth whereof I speak. Under tremendous stress Brother Burden, Sister Gotzian, Mrs. Kittle and I bought the other half of the block upon which we are now located, taking the responsibility of paying for it ourselves. For this I was severely criticized, but I felt that we must have enough land so that we could put up our buildings on a simple cottage style, and God has blessed in this and our buildings now stand as a monument to that experience and are in harmony with what has been written in the Spirit of

---

96 Edward A. Sutherland, M.D., "My Sixty Years' Friendship with Percy T. Magan," *The Journal, Alumni Association College of Medical Evangelists*, March 1948.

97 Ibid.

Prophecy in regard to Seventh-day Adventist buildings."[98]

"The General Conference brethren are making things very hard for us here. The Lord has always thwarted their designs against the school in days gone by, and I have all confidence that He will thwart them again, but just at present on account of the Musgrave report, and their attitude to it, we are passing through the deepest kind of waters," he wrote to her in 1921.[99]

Other similar struggles continued even after the dedication of the White Memorial Hospital in 1918, but Magan's faith in the Spirit of Prophecy prevailed, and the College of Medical Evangelists achieved Grade A rating on November 16, 1922, twelve years after Ellen White had directed the church to operate a fully accredited medical school.

Magan rose high in the medical profession. He served on the Governing Medical Board of the Los Angeles County Hospital. A *Review* article quoted another journal that featured the College of Medical Evangelists as saying, "Percy T. Magan, who has not only accomplished remarkable results against tremendous odds, but who has also found time to respond to every call which organized medicine has made upon him,"[100] which included important speaking appointments as well as serving on important AMA committees.

This same article described the Adventist medical school as "the only school teaching scientific medicine in the United States emphasizing those phases of the life of the Great Physician concerning the healing art.

"The graduates of the College of Medical Evangelists are to be found scattered all over the world," the article continued. "They are at work in the vast territories of China, from the borders of Tibet to the Yellow Sea. Numbers of them who might be living in their homeland in comfort and affluence are burying their lives in the furrow of earth's need in remote districts of the great empire of India. They are to be found dotting the but-little-known fastnesses of the Dark Continent of Africa, on the utmost borders of civilization, and in this way treading in the footsteps of the great Dr. David Livingstone, who so nobly gave his wondrous life for the dusky sons and daughters of that then unexplored land."[101]

The board elected Magan president of the College of Medical Evangelists in 1928. He retired in 1942 and died on December 16, 1947.

"His strong personal characteristics of leadership went into his crowning work—the development of the College of Medical Evangelists—which today is a monument to his memory," wrote Sutherland in summing up the work of his close friend. "With the cooperation of his fellow workers, the medical college has taken its place among the leading medical schools of the country, and thus has been fulfilled the prophecy of Mrs. White concerning the institution. Dr. Magan's faith in this

---

98 Percy Magan to Lida Funk Scott, August 19, 1919, Center for Adventist Research, Berrien Springs, Michigan.
99 Percy Magan to Lida Scott, October 20, 1921, Percy T. Magan Collection, Center for Adventist Research, Andrews University, Berrien Springs, Michigan.
100 *The Advent Review and Sabbath Herald*, December 29, 1927, p. 18.
101 Ibid.

prediction was his guiding star. He bent every effort to accomplish it, and he lived to see the fulfillment of his dreams."[102]

Magan's vision for Madison and the College of Medical Evangelists was to see his graduates serve as part of the gospel ministry. "Now, it is for us in the medical school to train Lukes—beloved physicians. We are to prepare Lukes—evangelists—to accompany great apostles on their journeys. The men who come forth from the medical school must be those who walk so close to the Great Physician that they, as did that evangelist physician Luke, write again the gospel of the Master's life in their own. They must share in the spirit and sacrifice of their brethren who preach the word."[103]

---

[102] Edward A. Sutherland, M.D., "My Sixty Years' Friendship with Percy T. Magan," *The Journal, Alumni Association College of Medical Evangelists,* March 1948.

[103] *The Advent Review and Sabbath Herald,* November 1, 1928, p. 15.

Getting Back To The Vision

And so, for various reasons, Seventh-day Adventist physicians and ministers never found a way to work together in making physical healing and healthful living a part of gospel proclamation.

As a result, the world went its own way as though Adventists didn't exist. Spirit-filled Adventist ministers preached the powerful three angels' messages mostly to their fellow believers, as things turned out.

"I have been shown that in our labor for the enlightenment of the people in the large cities the work has not been as well organized or the methods of labor as efficient as in other churches that have not the great light we regard as so essential," Ellen White once commented. "Why is this? Because so many of our laborers have been those who love to preach (and many who were not thoroughly qualified to preach were set at work), and a large share of the labor has been put forth in preaching."[1]

Sutherland best summed up the full implications of following Spirit of Prophecy guidelines in a letter he wrote to Evans, president of the struggling young medical school at Loma Linda, in praising the contentious 1915 Fall Council decision to go ahead and accredit the College of Medical Evangelists.

"We have taken our stand on questions that were clearly set forth by the testimonies, questions which seem to be absolutely impossible to accept by those who do not believe the Testimonies, and we have seen victory simply as the result of believing and acting upon the principles enunciated by the testimonies," Sutherland wrote. "To my mind we do not have faith unless we do believe in something that does seem out of reach to the human mind."[2]

Sutherland himself went through a challenge of faith. In a speech given at Loma Linda many years later, Sutherland said he had challenged Ellen White on the church operating a medical school. He and Magan had just graduated from the University of Tennessee and felt it couldn't be done.

---

1 Ellen G. White, *Medical Ministry*, p. 301.

2 E. A. Sutherland to Newton Evans, November 24, 1915, Center for Adventist Research, Andrews University, Berrien Springs, Michigan.

"When we got through the medical course in 1914, I said to Magan, 'I'm going out and have a talk with Sister White. I'm going to tell Sister White some things that I've done that she doesn't know anything about in running a medical school.' Because during the four years that we were in medical school, the American Medical Association was trimming down the number of colleges. They'd already cut out more than 100 medical colleges, threw them out, and others they put in such a hard place that they dropped out later on and they intended to see that only one medical college should exist in a state unless there was a university and a private medical school and then they would leave two. They would not allow, as a rule, two medical schools in the same state. And they intended to bring the standards up."[3]

He also felt Loma Linda could not come up with enough money to pay for adequate buildings and staff. "Every time when I would tell her all of that wisdom that I had gained during my medical course, all of the things that I thought I knew about what it meant to stay in the Association, she would just come back and say, 'The Lord has shown me that the College of Medical Evangelists is going to be one of the first colleges in the land and that the products of this institution would stand the highest, and the result of this work would go all over the world.'"[4]

That was enough for Sutherland to put him on track to a growth-in-faith experience, as he related in his letter.

"To believe those things that are perfectly reasonable to those who do not believe requires no faith," he continued.[5]

In other words, going to medical school and building a world-famous medical center made perfect sense to young Kellogg, visions or no visions. Perfecting a conference organization capable of responding to the needs of a world field fit right into the high talents of Daniells. He was also fine with sending missionaries overseas, launching strong publishing and youth programs, and conducting great evangelistic crusades not to mention avoiding the embarrassment of debt.

"But belief in a thing that seems unreasonable to one who does not have faith in God's work and the Testimonies requires great faith."[6]

And building Loma Linda made absolutely no sense, especially to the American Medical Association. Magan's medical school professors felt he should devote himself to operating a successful sanitarium at Madison. Some prominent Adventists agreed. Kellogg could see that following Ellen White's directives would hurt his popularity in the secular world, especially the medical profession. Daniells felt that a spirit-filled ministry fulfilling the prophecies of Daniel and Revelation would be plenty adequate to impact the world.

"Many of us have very little faith that is genuine," Sutherland continued. "Faith is the substance

---

3   "Talk by E. A. Sutherland," transcription of original recording held in Archives and Special Collections, Del E. Webb Memorial Library, Loma Linda University, California. Transcribed on October 15, 1997.

4   Ibid.

5   Ibid.

6   Ibid.

of things hoped for, the evidence of things not seen, and yet I should judge that there are many of our brethren who cannot bring themselves to believe that Loma Linda will succeed."[7]

The medical school was indeed "not seen" at the time of this letter, and the same may be said for finishing God's work on earth. Just as bringing the College of Medical Evangelists to full fruition in 1915 required as much religious faith as professional medical skill, the same basic principle is true of completing the mission of the Seventh-day Adventist Church.

"You have the sure word of prophecy to rest your faith upon. So go ahead, trusting God humbly, following where He leads in this great medical reform, and you will see success and victory crowning your efforts," Sutherland concluded. "If at any time I can serve you in this great effort, that you are putting forth, let me know, and it will be a pleasure to do so."[8]

A great medical school came out of the unseen, partly because of crucially needed financial support from Sutherland. He and Magan did all they could to follow the counsel of Ellen White, and though they took terrible criticism, their work still lives and bears fruit.

History shows that exercising this level of faith, a faith in God and the guidance of His prophets, often involves sacrifices and persecution, but in the end this type of devotion and dedication will touch the soul and culture of the world.

---

7   Ibid.
8   Ibid.

We invite you to view the complete
selection of titles we publish at:

www.TEACHServices.com

Scan with your mobile
device to go directly
to our website.

Please write or email us your praises, reactions, or
thoughts about this or any other book we publish at:

P.O. Box 954
Ringgold, GA 30736

info@TEACHServices.com

TEACH Services, Inc., titles may be purchased in bulk for
educational, business, fund-raising, or sales promotional use.
For information, please e-mail:

BulkSales@TEACHServices.com

Finally, if you are interested in seeing
your own book in print, please contact us at

publishing@TEACHServices.com

We would be happy to review your manuscript for free.

www.ingramcontent.com/pod-product-compliance
Lightning Source LLC
Chambersburg PA
CBHW081925170426
43200CB00014B/2834